# The Iveagh Bequest
# KENWOOD

*Julius Bryant*

*The London Historic House Museums Trust*

**SAVILLS**

English⌗Heritage

# Foreword

*This book has been produced by English Heritage and is published by the London Historic House Museums Trust.*

*The Trust was established in 1987 to raise funds for projects and acquisitions at four historic house museums in London: The Iveagh Bequest, Kenwood, Marble Hill House, Twickenham, Ranger's House, Blackheath and Chiswick House.*

*These great houses are now the responsibility of English Heritage, but so long as public funding of the arts continues to be under strong financial pressure, there will remain a vital role for the Trust in ensuring that the houses are maintained as active living entities. We are greatly indebted to Savills and English Heritage for generously sponsoring this important new publication, a book which continues the tradition set by Sir John Summerson's notable* Kenwood: A Short Account *first published in 1953. The Trust would also like to thank Julius Bryant, Head of Museums Division at English Heritage, and the various staff of English Heritage who have helped to make it such a handsome and informative souvenir of a visit to one of London's most outstanding art collections and one of Adam's finest villas.*

## LORD HUTCHINSON, QC
### CHAIRMAN, LONDON HISTORIC HOUSE MUSEUMS TRUST

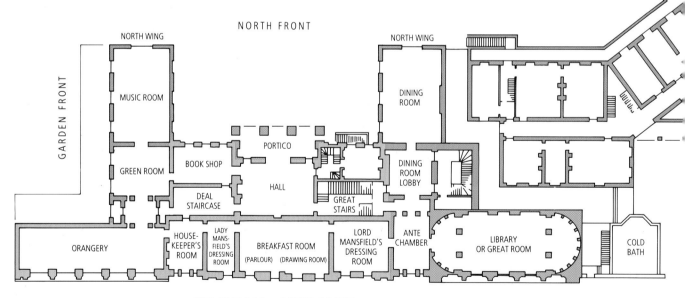

# Contents

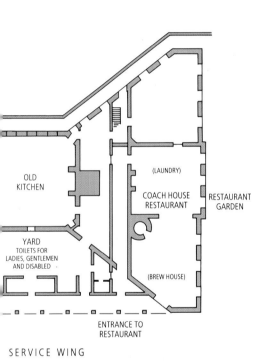

*Plan of the ground floor and service wing (all named rooms are open to visitors).*

# Introduction

THE IVEAGH BEQUEST, KENWOOD is internationally renowned for the collection of paintings bequeathed to the nation in 1927 by Edward Cecil Guinness, 1st Earl of Iveagh. Among the many world-famous works are a late *Self Portrait* by Rembrandt, *The Guitar Player* by Vermeer and *Mary, Countess Howe* by Gainsborough, together with exquisite paintings by Hals, Van Dyck, Reynolds, Romney, Turner and many others.

The collection is housed in the magnificent villa remodelled by Robert Adam from 1764 to 1779 for William Murray, 1st Earl of Mansfield and Lord Chief Justice. To the brick house built here around 1700, Adam added the imposing portico on the north front, a third storey, and the wing containing his breathtaking library or 'Great Room'. He encased the whole in white stucco and embellished the interior, all in his personal interpretation of the fashionable neoclassical style.

The villa stands on the crest of a ridge linking the villages of Hampstead and Highgate, and commands a fine prospect towards central London. In the landscaped grounds, open lawns stretch between lakes, rhododendrons and woodland, surrounded by Hampstead Heath. This idyllic rural setting belies the villa's proximity to the capital, which nearly led to the estate's suburban development, until Lord Iveagh saved Kenwood to provide a permanent home for his collection.

As a consequence of its varied fortunes Kenwood is now presented as an art gallery within a historic house rather than as the fully furnished home of Lord Mansfield and his heirs. Most of the furniture Adam designed to complete his decorative schemes was sold at auction in 1922, but the furniture collection today includes several of the 'lost' Kenwood pieces, following their rediscovery in private collections in North America, together with equivalent furniture from Adam houses contemporary with his work at Kenwood.

This book presents the first room-by-room reconstruction of the furnished house, tells the colourful story of its generations of residents, analyses its architectural importance and provides an introduction to the landscaped grounds. It also includes a history of the collections since Kenwood opened in 1928, and a description of some of the principal works of art. A full list of the items in the collection is available in the accompanying handlist.

## Chapter One

# THE FURNISHED INTERIOR

The floor plan of Kenwood remains essentially unchanged since the house was rebuilt around 1700, but for the addition of the library wing and third storey by Robert Adam from 1764 to 1779 and the two white brick wings by George Saunders a generation later (1793–96). The original house continued in use as the domestic apartments, while these later additions on the ground floor provided two suites of reception rooms. During the residence of the 1st Earl of Mansfield from 1754 to 1793 the family rooms appear to have been divided vertically on two storeys, with Lord Mansfield's bedchamber, dressing room and library to the east, and Lady Mansfield's domain adjacent to the orangery and original service wing, to the west. This distinction did not survive into the nineteenth century, after the new dining room and service wing were built to the east. The only significant alterations made to the original plan were the removal of a dividing wall between two rooms on the south front around 1815–17, and the alignment of doors between 1925 and 1928 when Kenwood was converted for use as a public art gallery.

Sadly, nearly all Kenwood's original contents are now missing. The paintings and furniture arranged by the 1st Earl of Mansfield and Robert Adam remained until 1922 only to be dispersed when Kenwood was stripped at auction. Fortunately, some of the finest works were retained by the Mansfield family for display at Scone Palace. A further misfortune is the lack of any early formal record of the contents; they were not listed, room by room, until 1831. However, Adam's time at Kenwood is remarkably well documented, in the Mansfield family's archive at Scone, and in the volumes of designs by the Adam brothers, preserved in Sir John Soane's Museum. For the later history there are other architects' sketches, engravings, craftsmen's invoices and visitors' descriptions.

This relative lack of architectural disturbance, together with the wealth of documentary evidence, has made it possible to reconstruct the changing identities of the rooms, and so determine not only how Kenwood was furnished from around 1770, but also how it functioned. Even though the furnished home of the first Earl, his family and heirs has passed from Kenwood forever, these living rooms can return to life through research, limited restoration and ample imagination.

The room names in this guide are those used by Adam himself, except for the later wings and the Breakfast Room, which follow the earliest inventory.

# THE HALL

FACING PREVIOUS PAGE
*The Library or 'Great Room',
considered by many to be Adam's
finest room.*
PREVIOUS PAGE *The lions and
deer in the Library frieze refer to
the Mansfield coat of arms.*

The imposing neoclassical portico crowning Kenwood's entrance promises a handsome hall within, but the modest scale and delicate decoration of this room may come as a surprise. This elegant interior lacks the classical severity of Robert Adam's great entrance halls (such as at Syon and Osterley) with their statues, stone floors and decorative reliefs of classical 'trophies' of arms and armour. Adam may have intended something grander, for on his original plan for Kenwood it is labelled 'Great Hall', but by 1774 (when the plan was published in the Adam brothers' *Works in Architecture*) it is simply the 'Hall'.

## The Hall as a dining room

One reason for this contrast in character between the portico and the Hall is the late date of this room, 1773. Whereas the portico was conceived in 1764, the Hall was the last major room Adam designed for Kenwood. By this time his style had moved even further from the civic architecture of classical Rome favoured by the prevailing Palladian movement. A more immediate explanation for this difference in scale and character, however, lies in the relatively small size of Kenwood, and in the Hall's dual function, as both entrance and dining room.

The dual function of this room was only recently recognised. The key to this discovery was the central ceiling painting, representing the Greek gods Bacchus and Ceres. Painted by Antonio Zucchi in 1773, this roundel was originally complemented by a further circular painting by Zucchi above the mantelpiece, of the same size, representing Diana, the goddess of hunting, with her nymphs and dogs. This overmantel (described by Zucchi in his financial account as '*le repos de la Chasse*' – the rest during the hunt) was probably removed around 1816; its present whereabouts remains a mystery.

In the ceiling painting Bacchus, the god of wine, can be seen with Ceres, the goddess of agriculture associated with harvest and abundance. This allusion to food and drink, befitting a dining room, is underlined by the infants shown bearing sheaves of corn, apples and bunches of grapes. The overmantel painting of Diana the huntress was an equally suitable reference to food and provided a classical alternative to the paintings of sporting subjects traditionally hung in entrance halls and dining rooms. In this way, Adam integrated the custom of displaying hunting scenes and still-lives of fruit and meat in dining rooms into his neoclassical scheme.

Decorative motifs further reveal the entrance hall's alternative use. The references to arms and armour, traditional in halls to allude to the

OPPOSITE *In May 1773
George Burns submitted his
account for 'a statuary Marble
Chimney Piece in the Dining
Room . . . from the Design of the
Messrs Adam.' Burns'
description corresponds exactly
with the chimneypiece in the
Hall, in which Bacchus, the
Greek god of wine, may be seen
between garlands of vine leaves.
The original overmantel by
Zucchi, representing Diana
hunting (an appropriate reference
in a dining room and entrance
hall) is now lost. Here its place
is taken by Sir Joshua Reynolds'
painting* Venus chiding
Cupid for learning to cast
accounts *of 1771.*

owner's military might, are outshone as the theme of food, drink and plenty continues. The painted ceiling roundel is encircled by a grape-laden vine modelled in stucco. Beyond the outer circle of decorative mouldings on the ceiling may be seen crescent-shaped shields, as carried by the *peltast* soldiers of classical Greece. But instead of spears, pine cone staffs are crossed behind, and allude to Bacchus, for they represent his *thyrsus* (staff); one of these may be seen in the Zucchi painting. The circular plaster reliefs include the triumph of Bacchus (a procession led by Bacchus's drunken tutor Silenus) and a banquet (possibly showing Bacchus and Ariadne) while the six painted ovals depict dancing Bacchantes (the god of wine's devotees) holding cymbals, tambourines and garlands. Like the central roundel, they were painted on paper by Zucchi and then applied direct to the plaster ceiling.

Adam's design for this ceiling, dated 18 January 1773, survives in Sir John Soane's Museum. However, as it includes none of these references to Bacchus, it presumably predates the decision to make the Hall double as a dining room. The colour scheme today is based on paint-scrapes taken in 1973; an account survives for a more colourful scheme, but as no traces were found, this must have been either a rejected trial, or the scheme for the Great Stairs.

The marble chimneypiece depicts Bacchus once again, in the centre with grapes in his hair between garlands of vine leaves tied with ribbons. The two deer skulls on the mantelpiece would have related to the overmantel of Diana hunting; they also refer to the crest on the Mansfield coat of arms. Further deer skulls may be seen on the frieze below the ceiling (the design for which survives in Sir John Soane's Museum) alternating with rams' heads which may also refer to Bacchus. They would have comple-mented the paired ox skull motifs on the original

architraves around the doors, carved by Sefferin Nelson to Adam's design in 1772. They were removed around 1816 and the present architraves contrast with Adam's original decoration, being heavier and more traditional (the so-called 'egg and dart' moulding).

The arrangement of doors has changed since Adam's time, when symmetry complemented this rich vocabulary of decoration to create a sense of overall unity. Originally, three doorways faced the entrance and its flanking windows; the left one opened into a drawing room, the central door (where the niche stands today) led into a parlour, and the right-hand door was a cupboard. Today, both doors on this wall are cupboards. The door to the left of the chimneypiece led towards the original service wing; the door to the right of the chimneypiece post-dates Adam. In the wall facing the chimneypiece, the left-hand door originally led to the back stairs and the right-hand door still leads to the Great Stairs. Many other alterations were made around 1816 when the exterior wall had to be repaired because of dry rot. The lengthy account for work done from 1815 to 1817 includes 'New naked flooring of oak – & new deal floor . . . New Dado & Base to nearly two thirds of the Room' and the creation of the central niche.

Today, the dual function of the Hall sounds most inconvenient but it was probably only used for special occasions. Earlier accounts and annotations to Adam's designs reveal that the Parlour on the south front initially served as Lord Mansfield's dining room. Evidently around May 1773 Adam and his patron decided to remodel the Hall to double as a grander dining room, leaving the Parlour for family meals. Lord Mansfield's guests would have passed through the Hall, taking the door to the Great Stairs, and then assembled in the Library (also known as the 'Great Room'). When all was quiet, servants would have brought trestle tables in from the stairwells to create a grand dining room.

Dining in the entrance hall was nothing new; indeed, the idea dated back to medieval times when banquets were held in the great halls of manors. But the custom had died out by the mid-eighteenth century. In Adam's mind the lack of a permanent grand dining room at Kenwood may have been prompted not only by older traditions and economy of space, but by his admiration for French customs and etiquette. He revealed his sympathies when he defined a dining room in the first part of his *Works in Architecture* (1773):

To understand thoroughly the art of living, it is necessary perhaps to have passed some time amongst the French, and to have studied the customs of that social and conversible people. In one particular, however, our manners prevent us from imitating them. Their eating rooms seldom or never constitute a piece in their great apartments. . . . The reason of this is obvious; the French meet there only at meals . . . and as soon as the entertainment is over, they immediately retire to the rooms of company. It is not so with us. Accustomed by habit, or induced by the nature of our climate, we indulge more largely in the enjoyment of the bottle . . . these circumstances lead men to live more with one another, and more detached from the society of the ladies. The eating rooms are considered as the apartment of conversation, in which we are to pass a great part of our time. This renders it desirable to have them fitted up with elegance and splendour, but in a style different from that of other apartments. Instead of being hung with damask, tapestry, &c. they are always finished with stucco, and adorned with statues and paintings, that they may not retain the smell of the victuals.

## The Hall furniture

The furniture Adam designed for the Hall at Kenwood includes one of the best-known groups of its period, partly as a result of its publication in 1774 in Adam's *Works* (see page 76).

An invoice from the carver Sefferin Nelson for 'Furniture in the Hall', dated August 1773, reveals that two oval looking glasses in carved and painted frames hung on the piers between the entrance and its flanking windows. A design by Adam inscribed 'Glass frame for the Hall at Kenwood' and dated 20 March 1773 corresponds with the right-hand design in Adam's well-known engraving of the Kenwood furniture where it is inscribed 'Pier Glass in the Dining Room'. In 1773 Nelson also carved the well-known sideboard, pedestals and urns shown in the engraving. The oval mirror is clearly *en suite* with the sideboard, which features in the same engraving and is similarly described in the engraving as being 'in the Dining Room'. This important group of neoclassical furniture would have stood on the short wall opposite the fireplace, but it may have been more frequently used for 'family' dining in the Parlour. Certainly it was in the Hall by 1815, when the accounts for work in the 'Entrance' record 'Rails & Legs of Sideboard – and 2 pedestals and vases – painted Oak'. Happily, most of the sideboard suite has been rediscovered and gradually reassembled at Kenwood in recent years from private collections in North America. It may now be seen in the Breakfast Room.

First-hand accounts of this room are all too rare, but in April 1776 Samuel Curwen, the exiled loyalist from Salem, Massachusetts, noted on a visit to Kenwood: 'The house elegant, not large:– the centre is a noble portico, the walls of the hall, saloon, chambers, etc., covered with paper of India or Chinese figures. . . . In the hall are two tables of jet-black marble. The walls hung with portraits of Lord Mansfield and Lady, who was a daughter of Finch, Earl of Nottingham.' The portrait of Mansfield by Reynolds, and its companion by Martin, showing Lady Mansfield seated in the Kenwood library, may now be seen at Scone Palace, Perth.

The next known account, in Daniel Lysons' *Environs of London* (1795) dates from the second Earl's time, but may record an unchanged arrangement of sculpture in the hall. After noting the bust of the first Earl by Nollekens in the Library, Lysons cites another, by Rysbrack: 'There is another bust of his Lordship, when young, in the hall, one of Sir Isaac Newton, and the antique bust of Homer, in white marble, which was bequeathed to Lord Mansfield by Pope. The paintings in the hall are by Rebecca.' The latter item is a mis-attribution of the ceiling paintings by Zucchi. The bust by Rysbrack, together with those of Newton and Homer, are preserved at Scone.

The furniture in the Hall also included four low stools, probably arranged along the wall facing the entrance, one between each door. These may have been intended for servants. As Adam explained in his *Works*: 'The hall, both in our houses and in those of France, is a spacious apartment, intended as a room of access where servants in livery attend.' His views were later echoed in Thomas Sheraton's *Cabinet Dictionary* (1803): 'The hall is a general, or ought to be a general opening to all the principal apartments. . . . The furniture of a hall should therefore be bold, massive and simple. Yet noble in appearance, and introductory to the rest.' The four hall stools are still untraced, but were photographed in 1913.

*The ceiling roundel painted by Antonio Zucchi in 1773 represents Bacchus and Ceres, the Greek goddess of agriculture.*

*Sefferin Nelson supplied two oval looking glasses for the Hall in 1773. Adam published his design the following year in the second part of his* Works in Architecture *(1774), which is devoted to Kenwood.*

*The most extraordinary design by Adam for Kenwood reveals his versatility as both architect and interior decorator. Inscribed 'Eparge for Lord Mansfield', this drawing represents a fantastic centrepiece, or epergne, for the dining table, in which flowers and fruit would have been displayed. Unfortunately there is no record of it ever being commissioned, presumably in silver. (By courtesy of the Trustees of Sir John Soane's Museum)*

RIGHT *One of two magnificent neoclassical stools in the Hall today, after a design by Adam for the Earl of Shelburne, c.1768. Stools from the same set may be seen in the mausoleum at Bowood. As with the lost originals they replace at Kenwood, the small scale seems to increase the height of the Hall. This is one of many examples of the subtle means through which Adam remodelled the earlier house.*

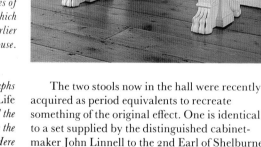

BELOW *Photographs taken for* Country Life *magazine in 1913 record the furnished interiors before the contents were sold in 1922. Here the wine cooler designed by Adam as part of his sideboard suite is used as a jardinière; it is now at Luton Hoo and the four stools (one of which is shown here) remain untraced.*

The two stools now in the hall were recently acquired as period equivalents to recreate something of the original effect. One is identical to a set supplied by the distinguished cabinet-maker John Linnell to the 2nd Earl of Shelburne around 1768, now in the mausoleum at Bowood, while the other is a later eighteenth-century copy, probably by an estate carpenter. Adam's design for Lord Shelburne's stools, based on a Roman sarcophagus, is in Sir John Soane's Museum.

The earliest inventory of Kenwood, drawn up in 1831, provides evidence of the Hall's soft furnishings. A '*large hearth rug 9ft by 3ft 6*' lay on the '*square floor cloth 7yds by 5¾ yards*'. The windows may have been left bare in Adam's day, so as not to retain the smell of food when the Hall served as a dining room, but by 1831 both windows and the glazed doorway were hung with '*3 cotton window curtains lined with buff callico*' from '*3 brass rods and ends*'. The new niche opposite the entrance was filled by a '*Square pedestal with bronze ornaments and a beautiful vase at top in Recess*'.

## The general effect

From this wealth of evidence, we may reconstruct the Hall furnishings as they appeared in the first Earl's day. Portraits of Lord and Lady Mansfield hung on either side of the central door (today the niche). Facing the windows and entrance door they received the best light, and effectively welcomed guests. Below, four low stools were arranged along this same wall. Opposite, a pair of oval looking glasses in elaborately carved and painted frames flanked the entrance; tables supporting black marble slabs stood beneath. On most occasions the sideboard would have stood against the short wall (facing the marble chimneypiece) flanked by urns on pedestals with the wine cooler below. The chimneypiece may have been flanked in turn by Pope's marble busts of Homer and Newton on pedestals, with the bust of William Murray alongside, where the later doorway to the shop stands today. Remarkable as it may seem, the walls appear to have been hung with imported paper from 'East India', in the *chinoiserie* taste. Trestle tables and candelabra on pedestals would have been brought in for dining.

Robert Adam himself may have been among the first to enjoy dining in this magnificent room, for on 14 July 1774 an American visitor to Kenwood, Thomas Hutchinson, noted in his diary 'Dined with Lord Mansfield at his seat at Kenwood' and recorded six other guests including 'Adams, his L[d] ship's Architect or Planner of his fine seat'. Hutchinson subsequently wrote in a letter: 'I dined yesterday with L[d] Mansfield at Kenwood, a most elegant place, and the entertainm[t] as elegant.'

The right-hand door in the wall opposite the chimneypiece leads further into the original reception suite and principal apartments.

# THE GREAT STAIRS

The 'Great Stairs' (as this room is described in Adam's published plan of Kenwood) were originally conceived on an even grander scale. In his first plan Adam set the stairs further back, beyond a screen of columns and pilasters, rather than to one side. Daylight would have poured down from the landing above through a grand Venetian window (comprising a tall central window flanked by two smaller ones). The intended stairs would have begun where the room ends today, at the far wall, and would have penetrated into the area now occupied by the Dining Room lobby and part of the Ante Chamber beyond.

The change in plan, resulting in the relatively modest stairwell we see today, was probably prompted by a change in the location of the main reception room in the house. Instead of ascending to the main rooms on the first floor, the *piano nobile*, as was customary in grand houses, Lord Mansfield's guests would have passed by this staircase, and on to the celebrated library or 'Great Room' added on the ground floor by Adam. The proposed screen was not abandoned altogether, but was built in the next room, the Ante Chamber to the Great Room, which gained in size on the drawing-board as the stairs were brought forward.

The Great Stairs we see today were clearly intended primarily for show, to be admired by guests as they walked towards the right door in the far wall to enter the Ante Chamber. In Adam's day the left door led into the 'Back Court' (complete with a water closet). The door in the left-hand wall, below the stairs, led to the original 'Breakfast Room' or 'Small Parlour' (see plan on page 47) while the door opposite originally opened into Lord Mansfield's Dressing Room. Both these doors are now closed to the public, but they remind us that Lord Mansfield could have used the Great Stairs to descend from his bedroom on the first floor, if he chose not to encounter servants on the adjacent back stairs (also closed to the public).

The crowning feature of Adam's 'Great Stairs' no longer survives. In his account for work done to the 'Best Staircase' in 1768–9, the decorative plasterer Joseph Rose specified: 'Flowers in Center of Ceiling two feet Diamr' together with charges to 'Frame Molding to Panels' and 'Run ye Cornice underlanding'. A particularly ingenious feature is the way the landing skirting merges with the dado and ultimately with the cornice. Adam's design for the ceiling, dated 1767, survives in Sir John Soane's Museum. Most of Rose's decorative plasterwork was removed after 1796 when Lord Mansfield's heir added the two brick wings flanking the entrance facade. At this time the

*The staircase balustrade provides a decorative screen which visitors pass on their way to The Great Room.*

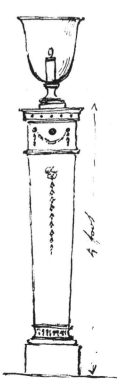

*Four 'terms' and lanterns provided candlelight in the relative gloom of the stair, and were probably moved into the entrance hall when it served as a dining room. Adam's design is inscribed 'A Term as wanted for the Great Staircase at Kenwood. Mr. Nelson is to make one Compleat, & if that is liked he is to do 3 more.' Sefferin Nelson was Adam's principal furniture carver at Kenwood. The present whereabouts of the terms is unknown. (By courtesy of the Trustees of Sir John Soane's Museum)*

window on the landing would have been filled, necessitating the creation of the present skylight. Some of Adam's ceiling initially survived, for an account for work done 1815–17 includes 'Several of the Ornaments restored to Staircase Ceiling'.

The open wrought-iron balustrade, mahogany handrail and carved staircase all remain as Adam intended, but for the addition (also around 1816) of a 'Cast Iron Column to strengthen Stairs'. The column remains and betrays the inadequate construction of this staircase, partly resulting from Adam's re-use of timbers from the older house. One of the walls had to be completely rebuilt from the cellars up in the 1950s. The same account for work done 1815–17 also includes 'Part of floor new – the rest relaid . . . Balusters gilt & bronzed'.

The anthemion (honeysuckle) motifs in the balustrade are noticeably sharper and crisper than the wrought-iron bars and circles; they are in fact cast brass, and were welded on by William Yates whose account for 'Smiths Work Done' at Kenwood in 1769 survives. Similar Adam balustrades may be seen at Osterley Park and Newby Hall. The brackets of the steps were enriched with carving by John Minshull whose account submitted in 1769 also included 'To Great Staircase Run of plain Water leaf in hollow of Door and Window Architrave', so confirming the construction of the window. The oak boards of the steps and landings provide a good idea of the random-width floorboards originally used throughout the house.

As in the Hall, Adam designed furniture for this room to complete the unity of effect so crucial to his principles as an architect. The evidence is his design for a 4-foot tall pedestal

supporting a candle in a glass. One is recorded beside the cast-iron column in an illustration in *Country Life* in 1913.

The right-hand door in the far wall leads into the Ante Chamber.

# THE ANTE CHAMBER

From the Great Stairs visitors enter a short passage cut through the exterior wall of the pre-Adam house (evident in the exceptional width of the wall, necessitating a door on each side). This leads into the only part of Kenwood wholly built by Adam. The 'Anti Chamber' (as it is named in Adam's published plan) was first designed by James Adam in 1764, as the vestibule to the Library or 'Great Room'. The Ante Chamber as built appears to have been little altered from James Adam's design whereas the Library was considerably revised by his older brother, Robert, prior to decoration and furnishing. It provides a revealing contrast with the entrance hall, designed almost a decade later. In this relatively plain vestibule guests would have paused before being led into the magnificent Library, the visual climax to the Adam brothers' reception suite at Kenwood.

The Ante Chamber played a crucial role in the visitor circuit. It is easily overlooked in favour of the Library. To reach this room, visitors experience a series of sudden contrasts, between the imposing portico, the more domestic Hall, the Great Stairs rising the height of the building, and the short passage. On entering this vestibule for the first time, visitors would expect to proceed straight along a fine marble colonnade towards the single door opposite. Adam intended the wall on the left as you enter today to be solid, with a full-length statue standing in a central niche; the tall double doors were only inserted in 1793–6.

The colonnade is, in fact, only a screen comprising two columns and two pilasters, painted to resemble marble, while the door at the end was originally sham. Instead of continuing straight to the single door, visitors were drawn by the statue's gesture and the opening in the colonnade to turn right and so discover the Venetian window. Here we can admire the magnificent prospect south, over landscaped lawns, to London. The panorama (today largely obscured by trees) would have struck visitors with astonishment, for hitherto it had been totally concealed from view.

### Adam and the picturesque
Adam realised that the inspiring view towards the capital was Kenwood's distinguishing virtue.

It partly accounts for the villa's location, far removed from the more fashionable riverside setting of Twickenham and Richmond, so favoured by courtiers who travelled into central London along the Thames. The architect made the most of the prospect, doubtless with Lord Mansfield's encouragement. Mansfield's mentor, Alexander Pope, had earlier advised patrons of landscape gardeners (specifically Lord Burlington) to make the 'genius of the place' their starting principle in just this way.

In the Kenwood section of his *Works*, Adam described the view from the terrace at Kenwood:

A great body of water covers the bottom, and serves to go round a large natural wood of tall trees rising one above another upon the sides of a hill. Over the vale through which the water flows, there is a noble view let into the house and terrace, of the city of London, Greenwich Hospital, the River Thames, the ships passing up and down, with an extensive prospect, but clear and distinct, on both sides of the river. To the north-east, and west of the house and terrace, the mountainous villages of Highgate and Hampstead form delightful objects. The whole scene is amazingly gay, magnificent, beautiful, and picturesque.

Adam's use of the term 'picturesque' provides a key to understanding the architectural principles that inspired this remarkable sequence of reception rooms, with their sudden changes in scale, light and decoration. In the preface to his *Works*, Adam described the first principle of his architecture in terms of the picturesque aesthetic then fashionable among theorists:

*Movement* is meant to express, the rise and fall, the advance and recess, with other diversity of form, in the different parts of a building, so as to add greatly to the picturesque of the composition. For the rising and falling, advancing and receding, with the convexity and concavity, and other forms of the great parts, have the same effect in architecture, that hill and dale, foreground and distance, swelling and sinking have in landscape; That is, they serve to produce an agreeable and diversified contour, that groups and contrasts like a picture, and creates a variety of light and shade, which gives great spirit, beauty and effect to the composition.

Framed within the Venetian window, Kenwood's grounds were intended to suggest paintings by Claude or Poussin, complete with an artificial lake apparently flowing under a sham bridge to suggest a riverside setting. As we look down from the foreground, our gaze comes to rest on the 'bridge' in the middle distance. Originally it would have proceeded to an inspiring panorama, with the Thames, St Paul's Cathedral and Greenwich Hospital. The latter was singled out by Adam in his description of the prospect because of his admiration for the Baroque architect Vanbrugh, whose use of 'movement, novelty and ingenuity' he praises in the *Works*.

OPPOSITE *The Great Stairs present a sudden contrast in scale in Adam's reception suite, which is typical of his love of 'movement'.*

*The 'Tatham' Pedestal, carved mahogany, c.1795–9. The design derives from a group of drawings made by C. H. Tatham in 1795 after two antique marble candelabra in the Vatican Museum.*

## Role of the Ante Chamber

Adam's description of the published plan of Kenwood leaves us in no doubt that this room was conceived primarily in relation to the Library: '*Plan* of KENWOOD. Of which the portico to the north, the great room or library, and its anti-room, are the new additions. . . . The great room, with its anti-room, was begun by Lord Mansfield's orders, in the year 1767.' The Ante Chamber is the exact width of the library but for the colonnade which serves as a dividing screen. Seen from the entrance, this colonnade frames the vista towards the Venetian window, so creating a sense of constraint that heightens the sudden contrast in scale. The same device will be found inside the Library, where columns flank the entrance. Ornate plasterwork provides a further foretaste of the splendours awaiting us within the Library, as in the ceiling and the panel above the doorway to Lord Mansfield's Dressing Room. Here a single door is carved to mirror the taller pair of mahogany doors to the Library. In his account for work done at Kenwood 1768–9, the plasterer Joseph Rose specifies in this room the ceiling, the lintels over the doors, the panel over the door opposite the Library, and the Ionic capitals.

For all these similarities the general character of the Ante Chamber is significantly different from the Library. In the Ionic columns, deep niches for sculpture, and the chair rail carved with the Vitruvian scroll motif, we are admiring the earlier style of Robert Adam and his younger brother James, a style still bound to Palladian traditions through the influence of their father, William Adam. The Ante Chamber remains closer to James Adam's rejected design for the Library, furnished with urns, busts and a carved caryatid mantelpiece (see page 18). In particular, the flat cove ceiling (the design for which, dated 1767, survives in Sir John Soane's Museum) provides a revealing contrast with Robert Adam's innovations in the Library.

Another key principle of the brothers' approach to architecture as interior design may be recognised in this room: unity. The repetition of certain motifs is a characteristic method they employed to achieve unity, whether on walls, ceilings, doors, carpets or furniture. In the Ante Chamber, Vitruvian scrolls can be seen on the chair rail around the entire room and on the outer border of the circular ceiling decoration of palm leaves and swags. We can also find alternating fluting and paterae (grooves and circular floral motifs) on the doors, the lintels above, and along the horizontal cornice dividing the walls from the cove ceiling. John Minshull's account for 'Carvers Work' at Kenwood, dated 9 August 1769, reveals that this one craftsman worked on the Ante Chamber, the Great Staircase, the Library, and elsewhere. Colour is a further key ingredient in the creation of unified interiors. The buff, pale blue and white of the historically recreated colour scheme in the Hall, Staircase and this room will all come together in the Library.

## Furniture

Although the Ante Chamber is exceptional in remaining largely unchanged (but for the north wall) little survives, beyond James Adam's cross-section design, to indicate how it was first furnished. An invoice records that 'three large Antyke figures viz Flora Teis and a muse' were supplied to Kenwood in 1771 by James Hoskins ('moulder and caster in plaster' to the Royal Academy) and his partner Samuel Oliver. These statues would have stood in the two tall niches still in this room and in the third niche in the former wall facing the window. The only recorded bust of Robert Adam was executed, in plaster, by Hoskins. An account for painter's work at Kenwood, dated 1815–17, includes 'Four Stools painted oak & covered with red leather'. This may refer to the four sarcophagus-shaped stools that stood in the entrance hall. The same stools also appear in the Ante Chamber in the inventory of 1831, with '2 arm chairs to correspond'. The painter's bill of 1815–17 also mentions 'New Hot-air stove . . . columns & pillasters painted in imitation of red porphyry . . . Window shutters, doors &c painted in imitation of oak'. The only item that appears to have remained *in situ* since 1831 is '*A bronze 2 light lamp & chain*'.

It seems unlikely that the Ante Chamber was used exclusively by guests at receptions, for the door facing the Library opens into Lord Mansfield's Dressing Room. As a vestibule it could have been used more frequently by visitors on business, waiting to be seen by Lord Mansfield during his morning *levée*. This would have made a set of stools very necessary. The Ante Chamber even has a fourth door, in the Venetian window, giving access to the terrace and the gardens.

*The third room in Lord Mansfield's new reception suite, the Ante Chamber was first designed in 1764 by James Adam (Robert's younger brother) and is relatively traditional in its use of classical decoration. Here visitors first discover the magnificent grounds and prospect through a 'Venetian' window. Originally the wall opposite the window was solid, with a statue in a niche.*

# THE LIBRARY

The Library or 'Great Room' at Kenwood is among the most impressive and memorable of late eighteenth-century British interiors, whether in civic, ecclesiastical or domestic architecture. This major example of the neoclassical style of design is considered by some to be Robert Adam's finest room. But it was even more splendid in Adam's day. Conceived to inspire awe, and completed by 1770 as the climax to Adam's reception suite, it survived virtually unaltered until 1922, when the original furniture was sold at auction. Happily the vast pier glasses and the three carved curtain cornices remain *in situ* and provide a flavour of the lost contents. Through continuing restoration and acquisitions the full splendour and meaning of Adam's influential achievement is becoming apparent once again.

## Robert Adam's 'Great Room'

Together with its Ante Chamber, the Library is the sole part of Kenwood wholly built by Adam. In commissioning this single-storey wing, Lord Mansfield contributed to a contemporary fashion. As the architect Isaac Ware noted in his *Complete Body of Architecture* (1768): 'We see an addition of a great room now to almost every house of consequence.' But Adam did far more than follow fashion, and realised the full potential of the commission. In the Kenwood section of his *Works* (1774) he devoted three engravings and their accompanying texts to the Library, the only room he chose to illustrate. It was clearly a form of manifesto. Adam records that the 'great room' was begun in 1767:

... and was intended both for a library and a room for receiving company. The circular recesses were therefore fitted up for the former purpose, and the square part, or body of the room, was made suitable to the latter. The whole is reckoned elegant in its proportions and decorations, and the ceiling in particular, which is a segment of a circle, has been generally admired.

In addition to being a library and a reception room, it was also conceived as a form of long gallery from which to admire Kenwood's grounds and exceptionally fine prospect towards London.

## The ceiling design

The unusual shape of the room (a double cube with semi-circular apses and a cove ceiling) is derived from ancient Roman public baths known as *thermae*. The novelty of the ceiling required the most explanation from Adam, for it differs greatly from the traditional coved ceiling (used in the Ante Chamber). He emphasised that it:

is in the form and style of those of the ancients. It is an imitation of a flat arch, which is extremely beautiful, and much more perfect than that which is commonly called the coved ceiling. . . . The coved ceiling, which is a portion or quadrant of a circle around the room, and rising to a flat in the centre, seems to be altogether of modern invention . . . it has been found of great use in the finishing of modern apartments; but, neither is its form so grand, nor does it admit of so much beauty of decoration, as the ancient arched ceilings; which consists of three kinds, the dome, the groin, and the plain trunk arch, such as that now before us.

Such readiness to challenge accepted conventions and return to classical precedents is typical of Adam, who sought to revitalise the revival of classical architecture by drawing upon his own field researches and on later styles. Rather than depend solely upon the pattern books of Vitruvius (fl. 40BC) and Palladio (1508–80), and on the evidence of surviving public buildings from classical times, Adam undertook his own investigations into domestic architecture. Most notable of these was the Palace of Emperor Diocletian at Split, whose Mausoleum partly inspired the Kenwood Library. The results, published in a lavish volume in 1764, provided Adam with new principles and a fresh vocabulary of ornament. These he combined with influences ranging from sixteenth-century Italy to contemporary France, via the neo-Palladian buildings of Lord Burlington, in order to bring about, as he claimed, 'a kind of revolution in the whole system' of architecture.

Adam's 'revolution' is perhaps epitomised by this ceiling. Not only is it a trunk arch, but it is decorated (in preference to the plain white ceilings characteristic of Palladian interiors) in order to create harmony between ceiling, walls and furnishings. Adam continues:

The stucco work of this ceiling, and of the other decorations, is finely executed, by Mr. Joseph Rose. The paintings are elegantly performed, by Mr. Antonio Zucchi, a Venetian painter, of great eminence; and the grounds of the pannels and freeses are coloured with light tints of pink and green, so as to take off the glare of white, so common in every ceiling, till of late. This always appeared to me so cold and unfinished, that I ventured to introduce this variety of grounds, at once to relieve the ornaments, remove the crudeness of the white, and create a harmony between the ceiling and the sidewalls, with their hangings, pictures, and other decorations.

Adam was mistaken in recalling that part of the ceiling was green, for paint-scrapes taken in 1969 revealed the original colour scheme, since recreated. The architect may have referred to the coloured design (still preserved in Sir John Soane's Museum). The site evidence suggests that Mansfield rejected this scheme in favour of another coloured design, which Adam's own craftsmen presumably used and then discarded. The earliest design for the ceiling, signed and dated 1764 by James Adam, is also preserved in Sir John Soane's Museum.

After the cove, another traditional treatment challenged by Adam at Kenwood was the more 'ponderous' type of compartment ceiling, 'of a most enormous weight and depth'. As Adam explained in the Preface to his *Works*:

These absurd compositions took their rise in Italy, under the first of their modern masters, who were in no doubt led into that idea from the observations of the soffits used by the ancients in the porticos of their temples and other public works. These the ancients, with their usual skill and judgement, kept of a bold and massive style, suiting them to the strength, magnitude, and height of the building. ... But on the inside of their edifices the ancients were extremely careful to proportion both the size and depth of their compartments and pannels, to the distance from the eye and the objects with which they were to be compared; and, with regard to the decoration of their

private and bathing apartments, they were all delicacy, gaiety, grace, and beauty. ... We shall only add, that from this mistake of the first modern Italian artists, all Europe has been misled, and has been servilely groaning under this load for these three centuries past.

## The screens

Adam further realised his principles (expounded in the Preface to his *Works*) in the two screens of Corinthian columns supporting entablatures that divide the body of the room from the apsidal ends. Whilst the columns flanking the entrance create a sense of constraint that effectively exaggerates the scale of the room beyond, the frieze decoration overhead serves to lighten the apparent weight of the entablature. As with cove and compartment ceilings, Adam felt that:

*The massive entablature* ... has been abused by the misapplication, ignorance, and want of invention in many modern artists. Nothing can be more noble and striking, when properly applied, than a fine order of columns, with their bases, capitals, and entablatures: nothing more sterile and disgustful, than to see for ever the dull repetition of Dorick, Ionick, and Corinthian entablatures, in their usual proportions, reigning round every apartment.

He explained that 'The frieze over the columns, is enriched with an ornament composed of lions and the heads of deer; the former being the supporters, and the latter the crest of the family.'

## The recesses

The only other aspects of the room that Adam considered significant enough to single out for comment were the mirrored recesses on either side of the marble chimneypiece. These, he writes, 'reflecting the objects that are seen from windows, have a most singular and beautiful effect'. As an alternative to windows on this wall (blocking the view of the kitchen garden and the public road) they direct our gaze back towards the grounds and the fine prospect beyond. Thomas Chippendale supplied the 'French plate Glass, in London Silver'd' for these recesses in 1769. A letter of security survives, in which Chippendale guarantees to repay the advance of £170 to Lord Mansfield in the event of this 'agreement enter'd into by him with Robert Adam' not being fulfilled. This is a very rare instance of a formal working relationship between Adam and Chippendale. Unfortunately the recesses were lined with bookshelves between 1815 and 1817 when the adjacent bookcases were lengthened down to the floor; the present mirrors and gilded decoration are a modern restoration.

## The original designs

Turning from Adam's own description of the room to the earliest designs we can see how these recesses were initially conceived to house books as part of a more sombre, Palladian library.

*A rare documented instance of the collaboration of Adam and Chippendale is provided by the mirrored recesses at Kenwood. (The Earl of Mansfield, Scone Palace, Perth)*

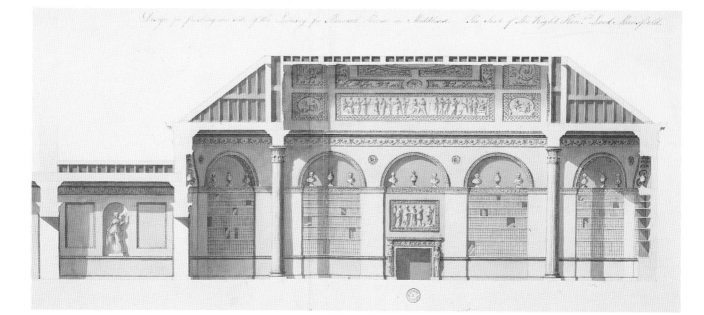

ABOVE *James Adam signed the earliest set of designs for the Library in 1764. Comparison reveals the characteristic qualities and genius of his older brother. This design also includes the north wall of the Ante Chamber. (By courtesy of the Trustees of Sir John Soane's Museum)*

RIGHT *Robert Adam's design for the north wall, 1767, includes a choice of sofas and proposes an historical painting for the overmantel, probably illustrating the administration of Roman justice. (By courtesy of the Trustees of Sir John Soane's Museum)*

BELOW *Robert Adam's design for the south wall reveals his integration of architecture, paintings, furniture, soft furnishings and books to achieve a complete interior. (By courtesy of the Trustees of Sir John Soane's Museum)*

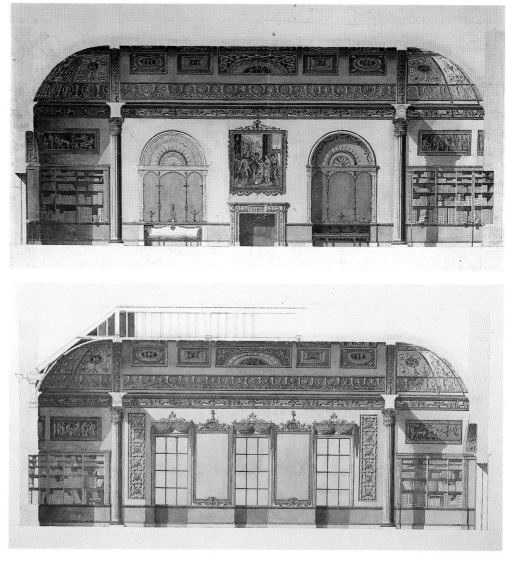

Comparison between these designs (signed by James Adam and dated 1764) and the finished room reveals the ingenuity of his older brother and the readiness of Lord Mansfield to accept a more radical approach.

The initial proposal was to give each of the apses a low, flat ceiling (instead of the present half domes) level with the top of the cornice. The central area of the room would have been more firmly defined, with the semi-circular spaces above the column screens filled in and decorated. The finished drawing of one apse shows how much darker they would have been. Over each of the bookcase bays and above the overmantel a recessed lunette would have contained two busts flanking an urn. No reference is made to the Mansfield armorial bearings in the earlier cornice, and a running frieze of the traditional Vitruvian scroll motif (as used in the Ante Chamber) would have linked the tops of the bookshelves. The chimneypiece would have been more sculptural, with the lintel supported by caryatids, while a panel painted to resemble sculpture or actually carved in low relief would have served as the overmantel.

Comparison with Robert Adam's later designs vividly demonstrates the 'revolution' he sought to bring about. Instead of weight, severity and homage to tried and tested traditions, he proposed a light and spacious solution that sparkles with rich, intricate ornament, set among subtle colours, united in a harmonious interplay of repeated and related motifs. Most noticeable, after his substitution of mirrored recesses for the two bookcases, is the inclusion of furniture (with a choice between two types of sofa).

## Portraits of Lord Mansfield

In the finished room a full-length portrait of Lord Mansfield painted by his fellow Scot David Martin formed the overmantel instead of the history painting Adam had intended. Martin must have exceeded Adam's dimensions for the commission, for he left no room for gilded swags beneath the fixed frame, as shown in the engraving. The portrait is now at Scone Palace, Perth, the seat of the Mansfield family, but a reduced replica by Martin may be seen at Kenwood. The choice of such a large portrait, in preference to a classical scene, must put the patron's modesty in some doubt.

In the portrait Mansfield is shown in baron's coronation robes, pointing to a passage in the writings of the great Roman philosopher and orator Cicero. The background is dominated by a bust of the Greek poet Homer (then attributed to Bernini) which Alexander Pope had bequeathed to his protégé. Behind, the imaginary spiral Solomonic columns (so-called from their supposed use in King Solomon's temple) allude to the wisdom of Mansfield's judgements as Lord Chief Justice. The marble

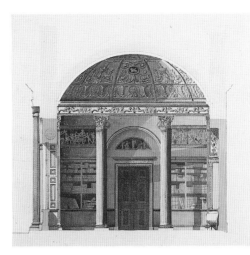

*Robert Adam's design for one of the apses. (By courtesy of the Trustees of Sir John Soane's Museum)*

bust of Homer is today at Scone, and its place is taken at Kenwood by an eighteenth-century bust of the Greek poet by Joseph Wilton.

A second portrait of Lord Mansfield could also be seen by visitors in this room. An article on Kenwood published in *The Morning Herald* in 1781 (itself evidence of early public interest in viewing the villa) noted: 'Between the pillars, at the upper end of the room is a bust of his Lordship, with this motto, *Uni Aequus Virtuti*; it does not entirely want similitude to the original.' This bust by Nollekens may still be seen at Kenwood. Together with the great overmantel portrait, the related central ceiling painting, the gilded frieze comprising the Mansfield lion and deer, and, indeed, the library itself, this portrait bust must have helped to endow the room with a strange shrine-like character. It would have exceeded the expectations of the great Lord Chief Justice's admirers whilst leaving less awe-struck guests in no doubt as to their host's appearance.

## Ceiling paintings

Martin's portrait of Mansfield is in striking contrast to the nineteen decorative paintings on the walls and ceiling. Unlike the portrait, they were painted on paper and then applied directly to the plaster. With their strong colours they were designed to be seen from afar, and contribute to the overall harmony of the decoration, without competing with the gilding, the red damask curtains and the carpet. They are further integrated through the variety of ovals, half-ovals, circles and rectangles that complement the rhythmic geometry of the room.

Like the roundel in the entrance hall, they were painted by the Venetian Antonio Zucchi. Unfortunately there is no historical evidence to support the romantic legend that Zucchi fell in love with the painter Angelica Kauffman (whom he married in 1781) while working at Kenwood. Zucchi's bill, dated 22 June 1769, survives, and specifies the subject of each painting in the Library. The central oval represents 'Hercules

*Detail of the Library chimneypiece, carved to Adam's design by John Deval the Younger in 1769.*

Hercules between Glory and the Passions *by Antonio Zucchi, 1769, the central ceiling painting in the Library.*

other idea than that of a dessert upon the plates of which are dished out bad copies of indifferent antiques'. Another contemporary regarded Adam as 'a certain compounder of ceilings' decorated with 'cheesecakes and raspberry tarts'.

The frames to the paintings in the apses repeat motifs used in the Ante Chamber. John Minshull's invoice of 1769 (already quoted for the Great Stairs and Ante Chamber) reveals that he carved the doors, shutters, architraves, bookcases, and the picture frame over the chimney. The plasterwork was executed by Joseph Rose junior, and far from merely framing Zucchi's paintings, it integrates them into the whole scheme. Rose's work varies from the bold anthemion motif (based on the honeysuckle flower) that runs around the central vault and the apses, visually binding the room together, to the sophisticated geometry of the lunettes in the mirrored recesses. The latter are typical of Adam's later style, such as attracted Horace Walpole's criticism of 'Mr Adam's gingerbread and sippets of embroidery' and Chambers' dismissal of Adam's 'filigrane toy work'. Through the coherent geometry of Rose's plasterwork, the abstract theme of the room, the semi-circle, is developed. This concern for structure and rhythm within the diversity of decoration seems to have been overlooked by Walpole and Chambers, and sets Adam apart from his many imitators.

The only real failing in the design and decoration of the library lay in the actual construction of Adam's ambitious vault. As early as 1793 George Saunders recommended that iron bars should be fitted over the entablatures to bind the columns together and so stop the roof spreading, and the 3rd Earl of Mansfield later employed Joseph Bonomi to build brick pillars in the cellar beneath the columns.

between Glory and the Passions', an appropriate allusion to wise judgement. The other paintings relate to Lord Mansfield but not through an integrated iconographical scheme; they are appropriate to his Library, just as Zucchi's decoration of the Hall enhanced its alternative use as a dining room. In the four lunettes we can find Justice embracing Peace; Commerce; Navigation, and Agriculture. The four seasons are included in the roundels, while the remaining four ceiling panels (*panneaux quavi*) contain symbolic figures of Religion, Jurisprudence, Mathematics and Philosophy. Above the entrance door Hercules appears again, only as an infant strangling two serpents. The walls of the apses are also decorated with classical subjects: The Aldobrandini Marriage; an Epithalamium (a marriage song); The Rape of Europa; a Bacchanal, and Minerva among the Arts.

## Craftsmen and criticism

Some indication of the mixed reception and influence of Adam's novel treatment of ceilings is given by his rival, Sir William Chambers. He lamented the 'trifling gaudy ceilings, now in fashion, which, composed as they are of little rounds, squares, hexagons, and ovals, excite no

## The furniture

For all the efforts of Adam's team of craftsmen, the greatest contribution to the original appearance of the Library was made by someone outside Adam's supervision: the King's cabinet-maker William France. By November 1768 Mansfield had run up a substantial account with France for work done at both Kenwood and his town house in Bloomsbury Square. Unlike other Kenwood accounts, it was submitted direct to the patron, and not through Adam. France received his final payment in March 1770, which provides an outside completion date for the Library.

In his account the more conservative designer took care to identify items 'performed from Mr Adam's designs'. These included '2 very rich frames for your Tables with 8 legs to Each richly carv'd ... and gilded', the three cornices for the curtains (still *in situ*), frames for the glass in the recesses, two gilded sofas to stand

*The marble mantelpiece is integrated with the whole scheme for the Library through its decoration with motifs employed elsewhere.*

in the recesses, and three gilded scroll stools for the windows. All the sofas were removed from Kenwood in 1922 and are still missing, but for one window stool which has returned but is beyond restoration. Fortunately, the larger sofas were photographed in 1913, so their rediscovery is only a matter of time, and detective work.

France also supplied festoon curtains (recently reconstructed from his accounts) and reupholstered eight 'gilt Elbow chairs' with 'your own crimson silk India Damask' to match. Each chair was finished 'with best burnish'd Nails with silk twist' and case covers 'of crimson serge with Silk strings to hang to the floor'. The two large sofas in the recesses and three scroll stools in the window bays were upholstered *en suite*. He also supplied two gilded pole screens to his own design to stand before the chimneypiece.

France's greatest task, however, was the installation of the vast French glasses, still on the piers between the windows. He charged Lord Mansfield for 'Myself & 4 men going to Kenwood to unpack' the French cases, cutting away the walls and fitting oak planks as wall frames. It took eight men three days simply to hang the pier-glasses. Two more then had to finish the gilt mouldings 'the French frames being very ill done' and because 'the gilding had been a good deal hurt by Unpacking & by Salt water'.

The French pier-glasses were worthy of Mansfield's 'great room', particularly in their exceptional scale. Samuel Curwen, on his visit to Kenwood in April 1776 (quoted earlier) remarked that the library 'contains the largest mirrors I ever saw, being seven and a half feet high by three and a half in breadth'. The largest glass commercially available in England in 1773 (the year French casting techniques were first used here) was only five feet six inches in length, and even then English glass still could not compete in quality. Not until 1780 did Adam install a large, single-plate English looking glass, still to be seen in the state bedchamber at Osterley Park. The installation of these huge pier glasses at Kenwood was all the more remarkable when one considers their journey by road; most fashionable villas at this time bordered the Thames at Richmond and Twickenham, where glass might be more safely delivered by river. These considerations, combined with the high import duties levied on glass, gave enormous prestige value to these pier glasses, and to the mirrored recesses. They reflected far more than light on Lord Mansfield.

For further evidence of the furnishings of this room we can turn to the earliest inventory of Kenwood, drawn up in 1831. The floor was then covered with 'A crimson color'd druget made and fitted to floor about 104 yards'. A correction notes it as a 'Cut pile bordered carpet made and fitted to room'. The border mirrored the anthemion frieze around the

ceiling, as in the later copy now on display. Before the fireplace lay 'A large size hearth rug to correspond'. The seat furniture at this date had changed little since France's day (but for the substitution of more fashionable striped case covers) and is described in more detail than France provided: '7 arm chairs white and gold frames, covered scarlet damask 8 ditto to correspond without arms rosewood frames 15 red stripe cotton covers for ditto lind with white callico 3 long window stools to match 2 large sophas and feather pillows to correspond 2 cotton stripe cases to ditto lind compleat'. The curtains were still scarlet, only now 'bordered with yellow silk & fringed' while France's two pier tables are described as having 'green marble tops 5 ft 2 ft 6', each one supporting a large alabaster vase.

An enormous quantity of additional furniture had been introduced to the Library by 1831, including six music stands and a 'Horizontal Piano forte by Broadwood'. The total valuation of £880 1s. 6d. given in the inventory confirms its continuing status as Kenwood's prime saloon.

## The furnishings today

Apart from the original pier glasses and curtain cornices, the Library today is furnished with appropriate equivalent pieces contemporary with Adam's employment at Kenwood. For example, the 'lion' suite was designed by Adam's rival, James 'Athenian' Stuart around 1760 for Spencer House, Green Park, and is noticeably more sculptural and robust than Adam's decoration. The pier tables beneath the mirrors were made around 1767–70 to furnish Sir Laurence Dundas's tapestry drawing room at Moor Park, Hertfordshire. Adam provided designs for this room, but not for these tables, which were probably supplied by Lawrence Fell

*Some of the original Library furniture (now lost) recorded in 1913. (Country Life)*

*The Library today.*

of almost all Queen Anne's Classics; and lists of subscribers to Pope's *Iliad*, and many such matters, all enlivening to some corner or other of the memory.'

Other, less presentable, volumes would have evoked less pleasant memories. Much of Lord Mansfield's original library was kept in his town house in Bloomsbury Square, until it was set ablaze during the Gordon Riots of 1780. According to James Thorne's account of Kenwood in his *Handbook to the Environs of London* (1876), 'There are also, carefully preserved in the library, the charred and stained relics saved from the fire made of Lord Mansfield's books, by the Gordon rioters, in 1780.' A 'list of books to be rejected from Kenwood library' survives at Scone among letters dated 1831–40. Eighteen pages long, it provides some idea of the collection, ranging in date and subject from *Petronii Satyricon* (1504) to *Bartholemy's Natural Philosophy* (1795).

## The complete interior

To appreciate fully the Library today, as Adam and his patron intended, we need to bring a vivid imagination to this wealth of historical evidence. We can readily picture this sumptuous room during a reception, with its crimson festoon curtains flowing from gilded cornices, down to gilded scroll sofas upholstered *en suite*, standing on a crimson carpet. Chairs would have been brought forward as required, particularly into groups around gaming tables. Candlelight would have flickered from candelabra brought in for the occasion, and, with the firelight, reflected off the mirrors and along the gilding. The ceiling would not have seemed so overwhelming. Even though the colours of Zucchi's paintings were rather more bold when fresh, they would have been balanced by the dominant crimson and gold of the furnishings below. Flowers from the gardens and Orangery provided the finishing touches, outshone only by the fashionable dress of the guests.

Adam succeeded in creating 'a harmony between the ceiling and the side walls, with their hangings, pictures, and other decorations', and the finished 'great room' attracted many admirers. In 1781, for example, *The Morning Herald* carried an article entitled 'A Peep into Lord Mansfield's Villa Caen Wood'. It noted: 'The Library is to most strangers, the greatest object; and if magnificent dimensions and harmonious proportions, new arrangement of structure, exquisite decorations and sumptuous furniture, are in request here, what is thus sought after, may be seen.' Adam concluded his own account: 'It is with much pleasure that I find my own ideas concerning the effect which this would produce, justified by experience, and confirmed by the opinion of every person who has seen this room.'

and William Turton. Adam designed the pedestals about 1765 for Dundas's London town house, 19 Arlington Street, and they may have been supplied by Chippendale. Like the Stuart suite, these pedestals are on loan from the Victoria and Albert Museum. The polished steel grate, featuring a patent ventilation system by James Oldham of London, post-dates Adam and was installed in the 1790s.

## Books past and present

The books we see today were assembled by Lord Iveagh. Adam took particular pains over the design of libraries and we can imagine a shared love between architect and patron in displaying the original volumes. Indeed, in a house with no gallery devoted to paintings or sculpture, this room would have provided visitors with the principal display of the resident's collection. For example, at the very end of Lord Mansfield's life the novelist Fanny Burney visited Kenwood with her eminent father and noted: 'We spent a good deal of time in the library, and saw first editions

# THE DINING ROOM LOBBY

From the Library, visitors should turn right and proceed to the second Earl's Dining Room via its ante chamber, thereby passing into this next generation in Kenwood's history. The Lobby was built on the site of the 'Back Court', shown on Adam's published plan of the house (see page 47); we enter through a double doorway in the north wall of Adam's library wing.

The 1st Earl of Mansfield's guests would have left the Library and returned to the Hall to dine. When David Murray, 2nd Earl of Mansfield (1727–96) succeeded his uncle and inherited Kenwood in 1793, he clearly found this dual function of the entrance hall to be both inconvenient and inadequate for his needs. This former British Ambassador to Paris added two further wings to the main house, thereby expanding Adam's reception suite to the north, while keeping it independent of the domestic apartments contained within the south side of the pre-Adam building. These two brick wings, flanking the entrance portico, provided the second Earl with a permanent dining room and a music room, each with its own ante chamber or lobby, linked by the entrance hall.

Adam had died in 1792, the year before the second Earl inherited Kenwood. The second Earl's choice of architect for these reception and service wings was initially Robert Nasmith, but he died on 30 August 1793. His place was taken by George Saunders. His work at Kenwood is indebted to Adam, but also reveals the influence of Henry Holland (1745–1806) particularly the latter's fashionable modifications to Carlton House, Pall Mall (demolished 1828) for George, Prince of Wales. For example, the most striking feature of the Lobby, the circular balustrade balcony overhead with a skylight above, recalls the Octagon vestibule at Carlton House; the coffered ceiling and plaster ornaments also reflect Holland's influence. Overall, the decorative mouldings are more detailed and less varied than in Adam's work nearly thirty years earlier.

In recent years this room has been known as the 'Marble Hall' but it is clear from a reference to 'Floor planed' in an account of 1817 that the floor was then made of wood, not marble. In 1817 the marble pedestal of a hot air stove in here was cleaned, and all the woodwork was painted to resemble oak. According to the inventory of 1831 (which gave the Lobby its present name) the room contained '*A sideboard table painted oak on 8 legs Scagliola marble top*' standing on a '*Floor cloth pland and fitted to floor about 46 yds*'. There was also the '*Dutch stove in white marble brass feet in front A large plaster figure on*

*top of stove*'. The latter must have been the figure supplied by Hoskins and Oliver to fill the niche in the former north wall of the Library's ante chamber. The statue, marble stove and marble-topped sideboard may thus explain the later name of this room.

The two doors in the east wall lead to a stone service staircase that originally descended to the second Earl's new service wing. With the guests settled in the Dining Room, and the double doors closed, this ante chamber would have been used by servants busily preparing to present the various courses.

The architrave around the doors to the Dining Room is decorated with console brackets and vine leaves. As in the entrance hall, these

*The 2nd Earl of Mansfield added the Dining Room wing in 1793–6, to the north of Adam's library wing.*

*The coffered ceiling and plaster ornaments in the Lobby reflect the influence of Henry Holland on the 2nd Earl of Mansfield's architect, George Saunders.*

vines allude to Bacchus, the Greek god of wine, and are appropriate to a dining room. Cornucopia, alluding to wealth and plenty, can be found above the doors, and in the ceiling spandrels. Both motifs continue in the decoration of the Dining Room.

# THE DINING ROOM

The Dining Room now contains the finest 'old master' paintings from Lord Iveagh's collection, particularly Rembrandt's self-portrait, painted around 1663, and the only Vermeer to be seen in this country outside the National Gallery and the Royal Collection, *The Guitar Player* of around 1672.

The architectural decoration is appropriate to a dining room, and continues from the Lobby. For example, the head of Bacchus can be seen on the marble chimneypiece with grape vines, as in the Hall. This chimneypiece was carved by the sculptor John Bingley around 1795. In the frieze below the ceiling we find paired leopards (a further reference to Bacchus, as they pulled his chariot) flanking urns (presumably containing wine) and alternating with cornucopia. An echo of the lion frieze in the Library may be intended here, but otherwise the room lacks any reference to Adam, and it may have seemed relatively plain to guests, particularly the ceiling, after the splendours of Adam's reception suite.

One principle the architect George Saunders shared with Robert Adam was a selective use of windows. As in the Library, a solid wall blocks any view of the kitchen garden and of Saunders'

*OPPOSITE* Portrait of the Artist *by Rembrandt van Rijn, c.1663, one of the world's greatest paintings, may be seen in the Dining Room.*

new Service Wing. Instead, the Dining Room faces across the portico to its pair, the Music Room wing. In a plan of around 1816 only the central window facing the fireplace is shown glazed, while the other two on this wall are blind.

The earliest reference to the contents of this room is in a county history published in 1816. The author, J. Norris Brewer, noted 'In the *Dining Room*, a large but plain apartment, is the portrait of Chief Justice Mansfield, by Sir Joshua Reynolds, from which has been made a well known engraving. The portrait of Lady Mansfield acts as a companion.' These two portraits are presumably the pair noted in the entrance hall by Samuel Curwen in 1776, and now at Scone. This 'plain apartment' was redecorated shortly after Brewer's visit, and an account for work at Kenwood dated 1815–17 records a lost decorative scheme: 'Walls painted in oil in pannels with corner ornaments &c' and the 'Doors, Shutters, Dado &c &c painted Oak' but no designs are known. The lost decoration in panels may have complemented Ibbetson's decoration of the Music Room (see page 36).

By the time the earliest inventory was compiled at Kenwood, in 1831, this room had been fully furnished. The many items recorded in here in the inventory include a set of dining tables (measuring 19 ft 6 in long and 6 ft wide when assembled together), two square pedestals ('1 for plate warmer lined with tin and shelves in ditto'), two wine coolers 'ornamented with brass', two plate stands and two dumb waiters. All were mahogany and were probably made *en suite* with the '*sideboards on six legs each front fluted and fluted legs*' still to be seen in the room today.

Twenty mahogany parlour chairs, their stuffed seats and backs covered with red morocco leather, lined the walls around a '*Turkey Carpet 8¼ yds by 5*' and a '*hearth rug 7 ft 8 by 3 feet*' on which stood '*2 mahogany fire screens with square shields*'. The screens would have matched the curtains. By 1831 the windows were crowned with '*4 rich burnished gold cornices*' from which hung '*4 Elegant scarlet cloth window curtains and draperies bordered with black velvet and yellow gold coloured lace drapery fringed*' together with '*4 white holland spring blinds*'.

The present grate corresponds with the description in the inventory of a '*Very large bright grate with spiked head & Vases*', and is presumably the original. The only other pieces original to the room are the '*2 large round pedestals painted wainscot colour*' which recently returned from Massachusetts through the generosity of the executors of Ellery Sedgwick and the Royal Oak Foundation.

Eight portraits hung in here in 1831, including the '*late Archbishop of York over fire place*'. William Markham was the father-in-law of the 3rd Earl of Mansfield; the portrait now hangs at Scone Palace. Its presence further suggests that

the third Earl and his wife may be credited with the full decoration of the Dining Room. This sumptuous room was completed by '*A large 6 light chandelier with balance weight & chain*'. The present cut-glass chandelier, acquired in 1965, dates from around 1810.

Some idea of the scale on which the second Earl intended to dine at Kenwood is provided by a brief entry in his account book at Scone: '1793 May 9 Table Linen for Kenwood £219.5s.' The only other indication of how the retired ambassador entertained in style is the remarkable collection of porcelain dinner services now at Scone.

Fully decorated and furnished (as recorded in 1831) this room would have been, quite literally, fit for a king, for in 1835 William IV and Queen Adelaide paid a formal visit to Kenwood. According to a local newspaper: 'At an early hour in the evening their Majesties partook of a sumptuous *dejeuné* in the banqueting-room.'

After dining, the second Earl's guests would have returned to the Library, or crossed the Hall to the Music Room. Today's visitor now returns to the Ante Chamber to find Lord Mansfield's Dressing Room directly opposite the Library.

# LORD MANSFIELD'S DRESSING ROOM

The main entrance to Lord Mansfield's Dressing Room cuts through the former exterior wall of the pre-Adam house, and dates from the addition of the Library wing. The room links the reception suites with the domestic apartments of the Mansfield family.

In the discussion of Kenwood in his *Works*, Adam explained that 'as many alterations were made, and many inside decorations added, in the apartments of the old house, these are reserved as the subject of another number'. Sadly, a further part of the *Works*, devoted to Kenwood, was never published, and so we lack any comparable engravings and discussion from which to recreate Adam's decorative schemes in the 'old house'. However, from the accounts and surviving designs we can deduce that he added chimneypieces, cornices, shutters, architraves and chair rails. From the ground plan published in the *Works* it is clear that these domestic apartments were divided vertically, on two floors, with Lord Mansfield's rooms to the east, adjacent to the Library, while Lady Mansfield's domain lay to the west, with the original Service Wing and Orangery beyond.

In the 1st Earl of Mansfield's day, there was a doorway to the left of the chimneypiece, near

ABOVE The Guitar Player *by Jan Vermeer, c.1672. The Dutch and Flemish paintings from Lord Iveagh's collection are discussed on pages 73–74.*

RIGHT Pieter van den Broecke *by Frans Hals, 1633. This successful merchant seaman is shown wearing a golden chain presented to him after seventeen years of service with the Dutch East India Company.*

the window, not to the right as now. In the north wall a jib doorway (traces of which are still visible) led directly to the Great Stairs. This second entrance meant that the Ante Chamber and Library could remain closed off from daily use. As Lord Mansfield's bedroom was on the first floor, he must have descended via the Great Stairs, or taken the adjacent back stairs. The Breakfast Room was directly opposite, across the stairwell (see plan, page 47). He then entered this Dressing Room through the former door in the north wall.

In the eighteenth century a dressing room also served as a morning reception room in which to receive visitors and transact urgent business. Isaac Ware in *A Complete Body of Architecture* (published in 1768, while Adam was working at Kenwood) describes a dressing room as follows:

A dressing-room in the house of a person of fashion is a room of consequence, not only for its natural use in being the place of dressing, but for the several persons who are seen there. The morning is a time many chuse for dispatching business; and as persons of this rank are not to be supposed to wait for people of that kind, they naturally give them orders to come about a certain hour, and admit them while they are dressing.

This use of the dressing-room shews also the necessity of a waiting-room where we have placed it. Though these persons are expected at a certain hour, they cannot always be admitted the moment they come, therefore they must have some place where to stay. When they are not there, it is convenient for the principal servants; who should have a room where they may be near their master, and in call.

Adam's Ante Chamber to the Library probably served as a waiting room to the Dressing Room in the way Ware describes.

Two designs by Adam for the marble chimneypiece survive in Sir John Soane's Museum. The sketch is inscribed 'Old Library' while on the finished design, dated 11 June 1779, the room is called 'the Dressing room'. These inscriptions indicate a third use of the room, and reveal it as possibly the last room on which Adam worked, post-dating the publication of the Kenwood section of the *Works* by five years. Presumably, it was only following the completion of the Library and the transfer of books from this room that Adam and Lord Mansfield were free to consider its redecoration.

The earliest description of the Dressing Room appeared in an account of Kenwood, published in the *Morning Herald* on 21 September 1781 (which must have been shortly after the room's completion). After listing several portraits in the house, the writer continues:

But yet, much more than these, indeed nothing less than *very valuably curious* are the three other objects to be mentioned: Dance's incomparable portrait of Garrick; the head of Betterton, said to be *painted* by Pope; and the bust of Homer, a *legacy* from Pope to Lord Mansfield.

The portraits and bust are still in the Mansfield family collection at Scone Palace. The memory of the actors Betterton and Garrick (Lord Mansfield had met the latter), and of his early mentor, the poet Alexander Pope, clearly made these prized possessions. As a younger son he would not have inherited any family portraits. Indeed, as he wished to dissociate himself from his Jacobite background, it is most unlikely that he would have hung any at Kenwood, but this need not have excluded his wife's family portraits. The article continued with a rare example of Mansfield's taste:

The room his Lordship usually reads in, is thus well hung; for besides the two before mentioned portraits of Betterton and Garrick, there are some good drawings of Raffaelle, and that modern Salvator Rosa, 'the rapid Mortimer.' The book upon his Lordship's table, and which apparently he had been lately perusing, was 'Weskett upon Commerce.'

Clearly, this 'Old Library' still served as Lord Mansfield's study and as a 'Cabinet' for his most prized possessions. The new Library or Great Room would have been far too difficult to heat for daily use, but was adjacent should Lord Mansfield require a book. In 1780 (the year before this article appeared) Mansfield's town house in Bloomsbury Square had been set ablaze during the Gordon Riots, and he had been forced to reside permanently at Kenwood, leaving his important legal library in ashes.

The room continued as 'Lord Mansfield's Reading Room' under the second Earl, and is first renamed the 'Japan Room' in 1817, when the third Earl's architect William Atkinson wrote to his patron explaining the delay in papering the room, as he was awaiting Lady Mansfield's return to Kenwood. The paper was mounted on canvas and battens, Adam's dado was repaired, a 'New Jib Door next to the Oak Staircase' was fitted, a new grate was inserted and the woodwork was 'painted to pattern'. The inventory of 1831 records the 'Japan Room' crowded with black and gold lacquered furniture in the chinoiserie taste, including a japanned couch covered in yellow silk and '2 window curtains to match fringed with a deep fringe draperies and Japanned and gold cornices' to either side of a pier glass. Presumably some of this furniture previously stood in the Upper Hall (which still retains its chinoiserie chimneypiece) before this room on the first floor was converted into the 'Billiard Room' between 1815 and 1817. By 1831 the Japan Room also contained twenty-six paintings and 'a Bust of a Dog in Marble'. The second item on the list of pictures was David Wilkie's *The Village Politicians*, purchased by the third Earl in 1806, and still in the Mansfield family's collection at Scone Palace (see chapter 3).

The doorway to the right of the chimneypiece leads into the Breakfast Room.

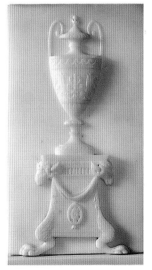

*Detail of the chimneypiece in Lord Mansfield's Dressing Room, c.1779–80.*

# THE BREAKFAST ROOM

*'Pier Glass in the Parlour' designed by Robert Adam. In August 1772 George Burns submitted an account 'To an Oval Glass frame, Carv'd & Gilded in Oil Gold . . . fixing up . . . in the Dining Parlour . . . £38.10.0'. The silvered glass alone cost a further £31.17.6. It was removed before the earliest inventory was compiled in 1831 and its present whereabouts is unknown. Fortunately the pier glass was engraved for the Kenwood section of Adam's* Works *(1774).*

*The 'Book Room' c.1913 when it served as the study of Grand Duke Michael of Russia. The bookcases were removed and the doorways moved shortly before Kenwood opened as an art gallery in 1928.*

This long central room on the south front was originally two rooms: the Drawing Room was adjacent to Lord Mansfield's Dressing Room and the Parlour lay on the far side. Two jib doors in the north wall gave direct access to each room from the entrance hall and they were directly linked by a doorway near the window in the dividing wall. The combined rooms are today known as the Breakfast Room, as named in the earliest known inventory, compiled in 1831.

Inscriptions on Adam's designs and descriptions in accounts reveal that the Parlour (as it is named on Adam's published plan) served as a dining room until May 1773, when the entrance hall was redecorated for this purpose. The Parlour probably continued as a family dining room in Lord Mansfield's day, with the 'Drawing Room' serving its traditional function as an adjacent room to withdraw to after meals.

The dividing wall was removed by the third Earl in 1815 when the two rooms became the 'Book Room'. Bookcases were installed and the cornice replaced at that time. The ceiling and window frames were also replaced, following the discovery of rotten timbers. The woodwork was grained to resemble oak and the 'Walls painted in oil with Corner Ornaments &c'. This 'Book Room' is recorded in a photograph taken around 1913 during the tenancy of Grand Duke Michael of Russia.

All that remains from Adam's time are the shutters and the Drawing Room chimneypiece.

Adam's design for the missing chimneyboard, inscribed 'first Drawing room at Kenwood' is preserved in Sir John Soane's Museum. A sash door survives, which would have given access from the Drawing Room to the terrace.

Some idea of the original furniture and of the lost carved decoration in the Parlour can be deduced from carpenters' accounts and from Adam's designs. For example, in the Kenwood furniture engraving in the *Works* the left of the two oval looking glasses is clearly inscribed 'Pier Glass in the Parlour'. It would have hung on the widest pier, between the two far windows in this enlarged room today. The sphinx motif on the pier-glass continued on the Parlour chimneypiece (now lost). The latter is described in George Burns' account of April 1772 as 'tablet with a vase drapery & sphinx's – frieze on each side with flutes, bands & tongue – 2 vases on the blocks – Trusses with double guiloche & flowers on the profiles & rafled leaves on bottom'. The carpenter John Phillips was paid in 1772 for 'making a frame for a Chimney Blind in the dining Parlour'. In August 1772 Adam examined Burns' account for carved cornices and friezes in 'foliage, leaves, bands & honeysuckle' for the walls with 'Door Cornices & Freezes enrich'd to answer the Cornice and Freeze which goes round the Room', all executed for the 'Dining Parlour'. Adam's design for the lost frieze survives in Sir John Soane's Museum.

The only other item on Burns' invoice for the oval glass is 'To a Table frame, Carv'd & Gilded in Oil Gold & the frieze painted blue colour . . . 19.2.9'. This table is now lost, but was presumably a pier table, made to stand beneath the oval pier glass. Clearly, George Burns was responsible for carving the architectural fittings, mantelpiece and the fixed furniture, resulting in a unity typical of Adam's ambitions. Burns is not otherwise known as a furniture-maker.

A richer impression of the furnishings in the enlarged room is provided by the inventory of 1831, which values the contents at £677. 1s. 6d., making it the most important room at Kenwood after the Library, Music Room and Dining Room. The Breakfast Room was clearly used for receiving company and not for family meals alone. It was dominated by an *'elegant set of rose wood dining tables 13 ft long 4.4 wide'*. Four huge mirrors hung on the window wall with three 'superb' pier tables each 'inlaid and ornamented with brass on 8 legs'. An idea of the colour scheme is provided by the description of '*4 buff coloured cotton window curtains and draperies with 4 muslin curtains lined with buff colour fringed and a burnish gold cornice in continuation*'. The four '*flower stands painted green*' probably stood in the window recesses, while fourteen cane-seated chairs stood around the walls, ready to be drawn forward for breakfast.

The sideboard suite in the room today could

have stood in the eighteenth-century Dining Parlour or in the entrance hall; the latter doubled as the principal dining room in Adam's day. The suite was carved by Sefferin Nelson to Adam's design in 1773, and was published the following year in the furniture engraving in Adam's *Works* together with pier glasses from the Library, Hall and Parlour (see pages 9 and 76).

*The splendid carved lion, to be seen on the mantelpiece, is a reference to the Mansfield coat of arms.*

# LADY MANSFIELD'S DRESSING ROOM

Lady Elizabeth Finch (1704–84) daughter of the 2nd Earl of Nottingham and 7th Earl of Winchilsea, married William Murray on 20 September 1738. She is represented at Kenwood in a portrait by Charles Jervas and in a marble bust by Rysbrack.

The Finch sisters were considered to be eligible brides, and when the Duke of Somerset sent his chaplain to make a suitable choice for matrimony the report came back (disguised as an appraisal of volumes in a library) that Lady Betty 'has ye advantage in ye fineness of ye paper and ye beauty of impression, but ye style is not embellished'. The Duke chose her eldest sister, Charlotte. Lady Betty's other sisters also

married fellow members of the aristocracy: Sir Roger Mostyn, 3rd Bt; the 1st Marquess of Rockingham; and the Duke of Cleveland. Only Lady Isabella remained unmarried; she commissioned from William Kent the great London town house, 44 Berkeley Square. Lady Betty's choice of the promising lawyer William Murray (several months her junior) was evidently regarded by some as a marriage beneath her station. It prompted the bluestocking Lady Mary Wortley Montagu to remark: 'People are divided in their opinions, as they commonly are, on the prudence of her choice. I am among those who think, *tout bien compté*, she has happily disposed of her person.'

Lord Mansfield's Dressing Room. In Adam's unpublished plan an additional door near the window led directly into the Housekeeper's Room and so on to the 'Green House' (the Orangery).

Lady Mansfield's Dressing Room would have been the centre of the domestic administration of Kenwood. She could have reached this room from her bedchamber on the first floor by descending a back stair (where the book shop can be found today) and then following a passage to the China Closet. This same passage connected with the Housekeeper's Room, Butler's Pantry, and the original service wing beyond. Ladies also used their dressing rooms to receive company at this time; from the entrance hall visitors could have been shown either along the passage or through the Parlour to gain morning access to her ladyship. However, as her room is only a fraction of the size of Lord Mansfield's Dressing Room (at the opposite end of the south front) it seems unlikely that it was the morning setting for all domestic business.

On a ground plan of 1814 the room is inscribed 'Lord M's Study' and the smaller chamber contains a water closet. An account of 1815–17 mentions the bookshelves in the larger room, which was then hung with wallpaper. This change in function can be explained by the conversion of Lord Mansfield's Dressing Room into the 'Japan Room' in 1817. The third Lady Mansfield presumably preferred her husband's larger room in which to display a love for chinoiserie and this smaller dressing room had to serve as her husband's study.

Today the Dressing Room is devoted to the history of Kenwood, and contains a changing display of engravings (principally from Adam's *Works in Architecture*), documents and photographs of accounts submitted by painters and craftsmen to the 1st Earl of Mansfield.

*Lady Elizabeth Finch, later Lady Mansfield (left) with her sister Lady Henrietta, c.1732, by Charles Jervas.*

Lady Betty was then aged thirty-four.

Little is otherwise known of her, apart from her accomplishments as a hostess and her burial in Westminster Abbey, nine years before her husband. But some idea of her interests can be deduced from the architectural evidence for this room. Lady Mansfield's Dressing Room was originally entered from the Parlour through a door to the right of the present chimneypiece, nearer the window. Today's two doorways are a later addition; indeed, the northern end of the room was a separate chamber in her day, entered through a jib door in the dividing wall. In Adam's unpublished plan of Kenwood this smaller room is named the 'China Closet', and presumably contained some of the Chinese, Derby, Worcester, Sèvres and Meissen porcelain still in the Mansfield family collection at Scone Palace. The Dressing Room itself evidently contained Lady Mansfield's own library, for in 1770 the joiner Edward Lonsdale was paid for fitting bookcase doors. The room was heated by a fireplace in the north-east corner; the present wooden mantelpiece is a later copy of the one in

# THE HOUSEKEEPER'S ROOM

Like the corresponding Ante Chamber to the Library, this room links the pre-Adam house to an added wing, in this case the Orangery or 'Green House' beyond. The room is similarly dominated by a grand Venetian or 'Palladian' window (the name given to the one in the Ante Chamber in a carpenter's account of 1770), so-called from its favoured use by the architect Andrea Palladio (1508–80). In his publication *Ruins of the Palace of Emperor Diocletian at Spalatro* (1764) Adam maintained that an arch over two columns in the palace Vestibulum was the true origin of this favourite architectural feature.

At Kenwood both Venetian windows include doors onto the terrace, and serve as the forerunners of 'French' or 'picture' windows. However, in the Housekeeper's Room the window is not so much a frame through which guests might discover and admire the picturesque landscape (as in the Ante Chamber) but rather a necessary feature to preserve external symmetry, a characteristic concern of the neoclassical taste. It seems surprising that a housekeeper should enjoy such a large window, in contrast to her mistress's dressing room, but her mistress probably preferred privacy and warmth. Lord Mansfield's mentor, the poet Alexander Pope, criticised the fashion for imitating Italian architectural features such as this without due regard for the British climate in *An Epistle to Lord Burlington* (1731). Pope observed in particular how:

> ... your noble Rules
> Fill half the Land with *Imitating Fools* ...
> Proud to catch cold at a *Venetian* door.

We have now left both the reception suites and the domestic apartments, and have entered what was effectively the beginning of the former service wing. According to Adam's unpublished plan of Kenwood, the Housekeeper's Room was entered either from her mistress's dressing room (through a door near the window) or from a door in the north wall (since removed). In this plan the 'Green House' could be entered from this side, through a door nearer the window, but in Adam's final ground plan of Kenwood this wall is solid, and access to the Orangery was only possible from the opposite end, via the garden. As in Lady Mansfield's Dressing Room, a north wall, opposite the window, originally divided the present room into two.

The door in the former wall led through a small room corresponding in width to the China Closet, and on to a second 'Housekeeper's Room'. Beyond this lay the Butler's Pantry and a passage to the Servants' Hall and Kitchen. Through such careful planning, decisions made at the Parlour dining table could be passed along to the humblest servant, and the machinery necessary to run this large house could be under regular supervision.

By 1808 the closet had been knocked through and the enlarged room had become the 'School Room' (presumably for the 3rd Earl of Mansfield's children) with a chimneypiece in the centre of the 'Green House' wall. According to the inventory of 1831, '*8 maps on rollers*' hung in here while the furniture standing on a '*Brussell carpet*' comprised two mahogany bookcases fitted in the recesses, a '*child's chair & stand covered with red morocco leather*' and a '*square piano forte*'. The simple decoration of the School Room was completed by a '*large shell and different ornaments on chimney piece*'.

# THE ORANGERY

The traditional name of this room is not original, for it is identified as the 'Green House' on Adam's published plan (and *Orangerie* in the French sub-title). An article on Kenwood published in *The Ambulator* in 1780 makes special mention of its contents: 'The green house also is superb, and contains a very large collection of curious and exotic plants, trees &c.' Unfortunately, we have no record of the various plants in this conservatory at that time, but we may imagine tubs of orange trees, peach trees and myrtles, brought in from the terrace in winter, crowded together with geraniums, sweet marjorams and lavender. As well as being a practical protection for exotic plants, this garden room would have fulfilled a similar role to a long gallery in a Jacobean house, in which family and friends might promenade during wet weather, admiring the fine prospects across the grounds, whilst enjoying the additional benefits of rich colour, scent and fruit.

Orangeries became particularly popular in England after the accession to the crown of the Dutch Royal House of Orange in 1689. The exotic citrus fruit presented a political symbol of the owner's affiliation, and a status symbol of his or her wealth. However, oranges were not sufficiently hardy to withstand English frost. The most famous precedent is the orangery at Kensington Palace, built around 1704–05 for Queen Anne, possibly by Hawksmoor. A closer comparison is the classical 'Greenhouse' built by William Chambers at Kew in 1757–61. Kenwood's own 'Green House' pre-dates Adam's employment by Lord Mansfield (indeed, the Library was built partly to balance this room and so restore symmetry to the garden front). However, its exact date of construction is still unknown. The exterior was refaced by Adam, but the earlier brickwork survives beneath, while the cornice framing the ceiling belongs stylistically to the first half of the eighteenth century.

Kenwood's Orangery may date from the residence of William Bridges, who owned Kenwood from 1694 to 1704 and is believed to have replaced part of the original Jacobean house with the brick building Adam later remodelled (see chapter 2). However, two avid gardeners, Archibald Campbell, Earl of Ilay, later 3rd Duke of Argyll (part owner 1724–46) and his nephew John Stuart, 3rd Earl of Bute (resident 1746–54) may have been responsible, as both took a special interest in the cultivation of 'exoticks' (see chapter 5).

Originally this was a free-standing building, entered from the garden through a door in the far end. The south-facing windows are far larger than one would find in a domestic wing at this time, but even so the importance of light to plants had yet to be fully realised and top-lighting did not become a basic principle of greenhouses until the nineteenth century. Lord Mansfield's 'collection of curious and exotic plants' would have been warmed in the winter by stoves, by an underfloor heating system of hot water pipes (the present system is little changed) and by the warmth from the Kitchen and Bake House built on to the north wall, as recommended in Sir Hugh Platt's *The Garden of Eden* (1653). The hot water for the pipes would have come from the Kitchen.

This proximity of the 'Green House' and Kitchen would have been for aesthetic as well as practical reasons. As the landscape gardener Humphry Repton noted in his *Observations on the Theory and Practice of Landscape Gardening* (1803):

at Caenwood, at Thoresby, and some other large houses of the last century, green-houses were added to conceal offices behind them, and they either became a wing of the house, or were in the same style of architecture: but these were all built at a period when only orange trees and myrtles, or a very few other green-house plants, were introduced, and no light was required in the roof of such buildings. In many of them, indeed, the piers between each window are as large as the windows.

The columns on the exterior were presumably added by Adam to reduce the apparent bulk of the piers. According to Adam's earliest plan of Kenwood, the 'Green House' could be entered from the Housekeeper's Room as well as from the opposite end; this internal access is blocked in his published plan. The 'Glass doorway' to the second Earl's wing is first mentioned in an annotated plan drawn on paper watermarked 1808. According to a note on the same plan the floor was paved and was three inches lower than in the adjacent 'School Room'. The window frames and glass were replaced as part of the third Earl's general refurbishment of 1815–17.

Today the Orangery is even more like a 'long gallery', for it contains the finest paintings by Gainsborough in the collection, particularly his early masterpiece, *Mary, Countess Howe* of around 1763–4. The suite of furniture usually displayed here was designed by Robert Adam for Moor Park near Rickmansworth, and made in 1764; it has been reassembled at Kenwood from as far afield as Ireland, New York and Washington DC (see chapter 4).

From the Orangery, the glass doors in the north wall lead into the Music Room lobby or 'Green Room'.

RIGHT *The Orangery*.

# THE GREEN ROOM

The splendid vista culminating in the Music Room is the work of George Saunders (*c.*1762–1839). It complements the Dining Room wing on the opposite side of Adam's entrance portico, as part of the grand reception suite (and additional family accommodation upstairs) added by the 2nd Earl of Mansfield from 1793, and completed by his executors and son following his death in 1796. Here guests would have gathered by candlelight to enjoy elegant private musical parties, including recitals on a chamber organ (similar to the one now occupying its original position in the Music Room). By day, the windows opened on to a newly created flower garden, where family and guests would stroll through the crescent-shaped flower beds. It provided a more intimate and colourful outlook than the grand southern prospect over sweeping lawns and expansive ponds to the capital's skyline, on which previous generations placed such emphasis. Through the tall, west-facing windows afternoon sunlight would have flooded into the rooms, while on wet days family and friends could have relaxed outside under the long veranda.

This 'Supper Room' is first named as such in a note of 'Colours for Kenwood Settled by Lady Mansfield Oct 1816'. By the following year it had been painted olive green. In the Kenwood inventory of 1831 it is described as 'The Green Room'. None of the upholstery or curtains were green in colour, but the painter's account of 1817 includes 'Columns done in imitation of green porphyry'. They would have paired with the columns painted to resemble red porphyry in the Ante Chamber to the Library. This ante room to the Music Room occupies part of the site of the old service wing and servants' hall, and must have been built shortly after the construction of Saunders' more substantial service wing on the opposite side of the house.

Saunders was only in his early thirties when he succeeded Adam at Kenwood, but already he was Surveyor to the Trustees of the British Museum and in 1790 he had published *A Treatise on Theatres*. With its paired Ionic columns and entablatures this ante room pays homage to

Adam's Library, rather than merely presenting a pastiche of his neoclassical principles. According to an early plan, niches were to flank the door to the present bookshop, just as they flank the doors to the Library.

As in the Library, the column screens frame the vista and so heighten the grandeur of the saloon beyond. But they also create a subtle, and essential, architectural transition in scale from the round-headed greenhouse windows of the Orangery to the elegant double doors to the Music Room. One hardly notices the internal porch to the veranda and garden, or the door opposite that gave access to Saunders' new staircase to the 'Pink Wing' of bedrooms upstairs (closed to the public). There is a notable absence of fireplaces, but designs survive for a heating system in this wing, with stoves in each room. In his extension to the British Museum Saunders reemployed the idea of column screens in the Townley Gallery, where he also used top lighting and dome ceilings, as in the Dining Room Lobby.

## Furnishings

Luxurious furnishings filled this room in the 3rd Earl of Mansfield's time. According to the inventory of 1831 there were '*2 fawn colord moreene window curtains and drapery borderd with black velvet and fringed burnish gold ends and middle ornaments*'. They would have hung to the floor when open, being draw, rather than festoon, curtains, for the inventory refers to them again as '*2 Moreen window curtains to draw on brass rod*'. (Moreen is a stout woollen cotton, not to be confused with *moiré*, or watered silk). Between the curtains on the wall hung a '*Pier glass in 2 plates and burnish gold frame, top plate 80 [by] 46 bottom 46 [by] 36 [inches]*'. The sea of furniture reflected in this vast mirror was dominated by a '*Round Table in Center of room richly inlaid with different colord marble and green leather cover to ditto*'. The entrance to the Music Room was probably flanked by the '*2 superb dwarf wing bookcases inlaid with brass ornaments part glazed with plate glass*'. Around the walls '*10 mahogany chairs round seats covered red leather & brass nailed*' would have surrounded the '*Brussell carpet pland and fitted to room*'. The inventory records several further pieces (with a total valuation of £446.13s.6d., more than half the value of the Library furniture) but the most conspicuous items were probably the most practical: '*2 Dutch China fronted stoves brass bound and marble tops*'. Similar stoves were added in the Dining Room Lobby and stairwells between 1815 and 1817, and two survive at Kenwood today in the bookshop. In the Green Room they supported '*2 large alabaster vases*'. White holland spring blinds protected the precious contents from sunlight, in a room furnished to provide a mere foretaste of greater splendours yet to come.

# THE MUSIC ROOM

The Music Room became the second most important room at Kenwood after the Library. The culmination to Saunders' reception suite, it was occasionally referred to as the 'Drawing Room' after its completion in 1796. Here, Lord and Lady Mansfield's guests would have relaxed after taking dinner in the Dining Room, or in the afternoon when it doubled as a garden room, after strolling outside. It stands on the site of the former Kitchen Court and the old wall skirting the Great Court before the main entrance. But for the continuation of the gilded frieze of harps from the Green Room, the architectural decoration is quite plain. Fortunately the early descriptions in inventories and travellers' guides conjure up a vivid impression of lavish furnishings and painted decoration in the early nineteenth century.

The earliest evidence is an account of Kenwood in J. Norris Brewer's *Middlesex*, published in 1816. After describing the exterior the author turned to this room:

The sides of the Music Room are painted by Julius Ibbetson. In different pannels are introduced various operations of agriculture, fancifully represented as performed by unattired children. Interspersed are views in North Wales, delicately executed. Over the organ the artist has introduced cherubs, performing in concert on many instruments.

Julius Caesar Ibbetson (1759–1817) had served as draughtsman to the 2nd Lady Mansfield's brother on the British Mission to Peking in 1788, and had toured Wales with her cousin in 1792. His decorative scheme for this room consisted of large painted borders, terracotta red in colour,

*The Music Room c.1913, showing the painted decoration by Ibbetson, and some of the original furniture. (Country Life)*

with clustered musical instruments and painted ovals, as described above. Whilst appropriate to the music room, this scheme may have been intended as a light-hearted 'balance' to Zucchi's sober classical decoration of Adam's Library. Sadly, the central panels within the borders remained unfilled, like empty picture frames, partly because, as the artist Joseph Farington noted in his diary in 1799, Ibbetson 'gave his employers a great deal of trouble – there was no depending on him'. Ibbetson found time, however, to sketch and paint dairy cattle in the grounds at Kenwood.

Originally an organ by Robert and William Gray stood opposite the doorway, framed by one of the painted borders with Ibbetson's musician cherubs above. A payment to William Gray of £105 on 24 February 1796 is listed in the 2nd Earl of Mansfield's account at Hoare's Bank and the instrument is described in the 1831 inventory as 'A Beautiful Organ in a Rich inlaid Case'. The organ's present whereabouts is unknown, but a similar chamber organ by John England and Son of about 1790 was acquired in 1987 to take its place. Like the other musical instruments in this room today the chamber organ is in full working order and may be heard at occasional recitals. The focal position of the organ meant that the window to be seen on this end wall from outside is in fact sham. The external fenestration also includes blind windows along the fireplace wall; these too are doubtless original, as a view on to the forecourt would have distracted guests from the garden.

## Original furnishings

Something of the flavour of the original room survives in the elaborate chimneypiece furniture, which may have been installed by the 3rd Earl of Mansfield, after he inherited Kenwood in 1796. A photograph taken during the tenancy of Grand Duke Michael of Russia (1910–17) records an overmantel mirror *en suite* with Ibbetson's painted borders, complete with putti cavorting amidst swirling fronds. There must have been two further matching mirrors opposite, as the inventory of 1831 records '*Pair large pier glass's in Burnish gold Carvd frames, Plates 100 by 49. A Chimney glass to correspond Plate 84–49*'. The photograph also records the panel of dancing putti above the doorway and curtain pelmets over the windows to match the harp frieze.

The inventory of 1831 includes the only known record of the colourful furnishings. There were '*3 Rich Stripe Damask Crimson Colour and Drab window Curtains with cornices in burnish gold*'. The striped damask continued on a '*Large square Turkish Ottoman covered with the same to match window curtains . . . stripe cotton case to cover the whole*'. There were twelve armchairs with '*loose stripe cotton covers lind*', with matching loose covers on the '*2 Easy Chairs*'. On the floor lay a '*Rich wove*

LEFT *Instruments in the Music Room today include a Broadwood square piano of 1791 and a harp by Sebastian Erard, 1811.*

BELOW *Detail of the classical decoration on the harp.*

*tapistery carpet with a key border 8 yds by 6. Large hearth rug 10 ft by 3 ft 6'* as well as a '*Drap colo$^d$. Druget pland all round the room*'. On the windows '*3 white holland spring blinds*' were fitted to protect the fashionable 'Regency' period furnishings from the afternoon sun. To illuminate the room at night there hung '*A light beautiful cut glass chandelier in center of room and brown holland cover to ditto*'.

The 2nd Earl of Mansfield served as British ambassador in Paris between 1772 and 1778, and formed an important collection of eighteenth-century French furniture (now at Scone Palace) before he inherited Kenwood in 1793. It is possible that the elaborate wall decorations and mirrors in this revival of the French rococo taste were considered an appropriate setting for his

collection. The Kenwood inventory of 1831 records a wealth of fine furniture in the Music Room. Judging from the descriptions, it was mostly French. The value of the contents of this room in 1831 was £762.4s.0d., making it the most important room at Kenwood after the Library (which itself had furnishings to the value of £880.1s.6d.). There were, for example, '*2 Beautiful Commodes Richly inlaid with brass, brass mouldings, fluted legs in burnish gold and fine statuary marble tops. Library Table with fluted legs on casters to correspond. 2 Corner commode cupboards inlaid with brass to match.*' The first two commodes probably stood between the windows, for there were also '*4 China cups and saucers on commodes in pier*'. The principal seating recorded in 1831 was a suite of twelve armchairs

and two sofas with white and gold frames, needlework upholstery, and striped case covers. Two armchairs and a sofa fitting this description are visible in the early photograph, as are tables in the French taste. '*14 cane seated chairs in black and gold*' were also squeezed in.

The view from the window includes a reference back to Adam in the ironwork of the veranda, for the design is derived from the banisters to the Great Stairs. Before the trees grew to their present height the prospect was crowned by the Dairy Cottages (still visible when the trees are not in leaf), resembling a Swiss chalet.

### The bookshop

From the Music Room, today's visitors proceed to the bookshop. This room was formed out of the back stairs and butler's pantry between 1793 and 1796. Described as the Ante Room in the inventory of 1831, it includes the only two remaining stoves. The inventory records: '*2 China Dutch Stoves bound with brass marble tops and base and fitted in recess's 2 varigated marble vase standing on ditto. Brussell carpet to match one in Green Room. . . . 3 Cotton Window curtains lind white callico.*' In this room stood '*Merlins Weighing machine compleat*'. Gainsborough's portrait of the inventor John Joseph Merlin hangs at Kenwood, where his Skeleton Clock may also be seen (see page 77). The second Earl's accounts (when he was Lord Stormont) include a payment to Merlin on 14 October 1780: 'Merlins bill in full. 7 17 6 for a Sanctorius Ballance the rest for Lady S. mending tuning harpsichord &c'. His repairs were not sufficient, however, for only months later the same account book includes under 14 June 1781 'Stoddart in full for a Grand Piano Forte for Lady S. deducting 52£ 10 for her harpsichord which he agreed to take'.

After leaving the bookshop, visitors should cross the Hall to ascend the Great Stairs.

*The Upper Hall chimneypiece incorporates genuine Chinese painted marble tiles. They were probably exported from Canton as a screen, for they are painted on both sides.*

# THE UPPER HALL

The first floor is identified as the 'Bed Chamber Story' in Adam's *Works*. In plan it mirrors the ground floor almost exactly, but for the single-storey Library and Orangery wings. Unfortunately, no plan of this floor is known, so the various room names and functions have been deduced from scattered evidence.

The grand chamber on the first floor now known as the Upper Hall lies directly over the entrance hall, and probably served as the principal reception room before Adam added the Library or 'Great Room'. It would have been equivalent to a 'Great Room' on the *piano nobile* of a Palladian house a generation before. Host and

*Only a fragment of the chinoiserie wallpaper from the Upper Hall survives.*

guests could have gazed out through the tall windows, across the Great Court and Hampstead Lane to the Bishop of London's forest. This prospect was closed to give the present sense of seclusion by the 2nd Earl of Mansfield from 1793 (see chapter 5). Visitors may also admire at close hand the architectural decoration of Adam's portico.

As a reception room, the Upper Hall would have become redundant following the completion of the Library in 1770. By 1773 the Upper Hall appears to have been remodelled in the chinoiserie taste, a style particularly popular for bedrooms, presumably because of its dream-like imagery. In that year Adam's specialist carver Sefferin Nelson was paid for 'Four friezes to Ch[y] Piece in the Chinese Room with Gilding ye same'. A design by Adam for the magnificent chinoiserie chimneypiece survives in Sir John Soane's Museum. To crown this focal point of the room, a garniture of Oriental porcelain would have stood on the deep shelf.

This chimneypiece is all that remains today of the 'Chinese Room', apart from a colourful fragment of wallpaper showing birds and butterflies among blossoms and blooms. An account submitted by the wallpaper manufacturer Thomas Bromwich to Lady Mansfield in 1757 includes '18 yds Painted Chinese Rail Border 18 inches wide' which may refer to this room. Fortunately, similar rooms from this period survive elsewhere, and provide some idea of the Chinese Room's lost riches, particularly at Nostell Priory, Yorkshire, where the State Bedchamber and Dressing Room were refurbished in the chinoiserie taste by Chippendale in 1771.

Evidence of a previous decorative scheme and of the room's earlier use for receptions is provided by a pair of oval pier-glasses with their tables, sold from Kenwood in 1922 but preserved in the Wernher Collection, Luton Hoo. Fortunately they were photographed *in situ* in the Upper Hall for the auction catalogue in 1922. They were probably commissioned in the 1750s from William France.

A design for the cornice now in the Upper Hall, inscribed 'Cornice for Billiard Room Kenwood Jany 1816' reveals the room's later refurbishment and function. A related account records 'Chimney Piece repaired and regilt . . . Woodwork grained oak'. Such an alternative use for a redundant reception room was not peculiar to the nineteenth century; at Clandon, for example, the Great Dining Room on the first floor was converted to a billiard room by 1778. In J. Norris Brewer's *Middlesex* (1816) the description of Kenwood points out 'In the *Billiard Room* are several good family portraits'. These portraits are presumably the same ones recorded in a photograph taken during the tenancy of Grand Duke Michael of Russia

*One of the more extraordinary examples of Adam's versatility as a designer is the chimneypiece in the Upper Hall, completed in 1773. The fantastical carved decoration on the chimneypiece includes mermen flanked by flying griffins or wyverns and a cherub riding on a shell drawn by seahorses.*

*The Upper Hall, c.1913, showing portraits of David Garrick, the 2nd Earl of Mansfield, the Duchess of Queensberry, Dr Markham, Archbishop of York, and Alexander Pope. (Country Life)*

(1910–17). According to the inventory of 1831 the room was dominated by a billiard table 13 feet long and 6 feet 6 inches wide, standing on '*matting to floor 10 yds by 6½*'. To either side of the pier tables and pier glasses the windows were hung with three cotton festoon curtains lined with white calico, and although their colour is not recorded they probably echoed the '*10 painted cabriole chairs covered green damask*'. Today the decoration of the Upper Hall is kept to a minimum, as it is used for temporary exhibitions.

*Kenwood commands a fine prospect towards London, which may still be enjoyed from the upper windows.*

*Anne Farquhar by John Smart, 1770, one of the collection of miniatures presented to Kenwood in memory of Marie Elizabeth Jane Irving Draper, and now displayed on the first floor.*

# THE FAMILY BEDCHAMBERS

Kenwood's fine prospects over the landscaped grounds towards the City are partly obscured today by the growth of trees, but they can still be admired from the three rooms on the first floor along the south front. The two end rooms must have been Lord and Lady Mansfield's bedchambers, with their dressing rooms on the ground floor below, reached via the adjacent staircases at each end. The middle room may originally have been used by Lord Mansfield as a closet and bathroom, as his bedchamber lacks any adjacent rooms, unlike Lady Mansfield's bedchamber. But for the mantelpieces, these rooms are the least altered from the pre-Adam house, with their early eighteenth-century ceiling cornices.

## Lord Mansfield's bedchamber

The room adjoining the Great Stairs is the grandest, with its deep bed alcove and egg and dart cornice. Here would have stood Lord Mansfield's bed, traditionally the most important single piece of furniture in a great house. A lengthy account submitted to Lord

Mansfield by the king's cabinet-maker William France in 1768 begins with a grand bed, which is presumably his. It describes 'a field Bedstead on a particular construction with good screws & posts, hinges hooks & eyes & mahogany vauzes'. The detailed description also includes 'Herringbone lace to the whole bed Olives & studs for head and tester & binding & tape for Vallens'. The tester was the top of a 'four poster' bed, around which the valance hung, with the carved mahogany vases at each corner. The material used for the hangings was Lord Mansfield's 'own Dimotty' (dimity is a stout form of cotton, normally decorated with figures or raised stripes). The actual bedding consisted of 'a crankie Mattrass filled with dry wool', with two white upper mattresses, a bolster, a down pillow, three blankets and 'a fine white cotton counterpain'. The furnishings were completed by the addition of two festoon curtains, also 'of your own dimotty' for the windows. In 1772 the carpenter John Phillips submitted his account 'for putting up Glass in his Lordships Bed Chamber'. A looking glass would probably have been fitted between the windows. Designs survive in Sir John Soane's Museum for 'Lord Mansfield's Painted Chimney' which may have been intended for this room.

Alternatively, the bed France supplied may

have been for Lady Mansfield. On 28 September 1801 the artist Joseph Farington recorded in his diary a visit to Scone Palace. There he was shown

a Bed frame and hangings in which the Earl of Mansfield, the Chief Justice, was born & died. He was born in the town of Perth, and after the death of his mother had this bed brought up to London. & he made it his bed to the end of his life, after which his nephew, the last Earl, ordered it to be conveyed to Scone Palace. . . . The circumstances of the bed is worth regarding as it proves that his affections were strong and that engaged as he was in the most weighty concerns his mind was still subject to these feelings in a high degree.

Lord Mansfield finally retired in 1788, aged eighty-four. A widower for the past four years, he remained at Kenwood until he died here on 10 March, 1793. He became increasingly bedridden towards the end of his life, when the reception suite and domestic rooms of the ground floor were neglected in favour of these chambers and the Upper Hall.

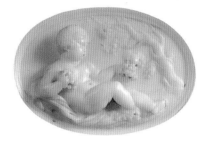

### Miss Murray's bedchamber

The middle bedroom is referred to as 'Miss Murrays Bedchamber' in Joseph Rose's account for repair works undertaken in 1769 and as 'the young Ladys Room' in a carpenter's account of 1772. An account submitted by the mason John Bingley in 1794–6 (which also includes his mantelpieces in the Music Room and Dining Room) refers to resetting stone and fitting in marble surrounds 'in Lady Mansfield's Room & Lady Caroline's Room'. 'Miss Murrays' must have been one (or all) of the first Earl's nieces, and 'Lady Caroline' the daughter of the second Earl.

### Lady Mansfield's bedchamber

By 1817 (according to an account for repairs) the end room with the bed alcove was the 'Blue Room', the central room was 'Lady Mansfield's Sitting Room' while the opposite end room was 'Lady Mansfield's Bed Room', with her 'Dressing Room' through the door to the left of the fireplace. The inventory of 1831 records in Lady Mansfield's bedroom '*a 6 ft 4 post bedstead and blue chintz cotton furniture*' with '*2 cotton drapery window curtains to correspond*'. A matching curtain hung in her Dressing Room. The most curious

piece of furniture in the whole inventory is recorded in her bedroom: '*mahogany case with phosphorous for obtaining instantaneous light*'.

The door to the right of the fireplace leads into the earliest panelled room at Kenwood. It probably dates from the beginning of the eighteenth century when the present brick house was built.

Like the Upper Hall, this suite of rooms is now kept relatively plain for temporary exhibitions, which alternate with the collection of jewellery presented by Mrs Hull Grundy and The Lady Maufe Collection of shoe buckles.

# THE DEAL STAIRCASE

From the Upper Hall, a jib door leads to the 'Deal Staircase' (as it was named in a painter's account of 1815–17, specifying 'Ballusters bronzed'). At that time this staircase led up to the third floor, which contained a nursery. Adam had succeeded in adding the third storey before removing the old roof. This floor is now closed to visitors. The lower flights of this staircase were created by the second Earl when the two wings were added to the north front. The previous 'back stairs' (shown on Adam's plans) were set back by the north facade, at the end of a landing and lit by windows. The inventory of 1831 records '*A yard wide Kidderminster stair carpet about 50 yds*'. These stairs lead back down to the entrance hall.

## Chapter Two

# THE BUILDING OF KENWOOD

For well over two centuries Kenwood has attracted admirers, but for all its fame, the architectural importance of the villa is not readily apparent. Among Robert Adam's major works it cannot compare in scale or contents with its rivals in outer London, Syon House (remodelled by Adam 1762–73) and Osterley Park House (1761–80). Compared to these suburban palaces, remodelled for great receptions where guests might parade through suites of rooms, Kenwood is a modest villa with wings attached. However, with its remarkable exterior decoration, particularly on the south front, Kenwood is the first complete example of Adam's mature style, used both inside and out. Furthermore, Robert Adam stated in his *Works* that the free rein he enjoyed from his patron, Lord Mansfield, was exceptional. At Kenwood he was not following in the recent footsteps of rivals such as Chambers and Stuart, nor was he seeking to satisfy a patron with strong preferences. This is confirmed by observing the development of Adam's characteristic style at Kenwood, from the initial designs, signed by his younger brother James in 1764, to the completion of the commission around 1779.

Kenwood's importance also derives from its fame in Adam's own lifetime; the architect made the most of the Lord Chief Justice's London villa to advertise his novel designs and materials. The second part of Adam's *Works in Architecture* (1774) is devoted to Kenwood, especially the Library or 'Great Room'; the engravings, text and finished room effectively presented a manifesto of his ambitions. We find him consciously reacting against the British Palladian school of architecture, developing his theories of 'movement' and his innovative treatment of classical motifs and subtle colour partly in response to fashionable aesthetic theories and to Kenwood's exceptional setting.

A further distinction is the extraordinary wealth of documentation that survives, including Adam's designs, craftsmen's accounts, and early descriptions in newspapers and gentlemen's travel guides of the period, as well as in the correspondence and diaries of visitors. People came not only as guests of Lord Mansfield, but also as strangers, as admirers (or enemies) of the great judge, or because they were drawn by the fame of Adam's work. Kenwood was only a short ride from central London or from fashionable Hampstead and, unlike Syon and Osterley, could be seen with ease from public roads and footpaths. Published descriptions continued into the twentieth century, and reveal that the fabric of the villa and its outbuildings have remained essentially unchanged since the early nineteenth century.

*Kenwood, drawn by Mrs Delany in 1756, detail. (National Gallery of Ireland)*

FACING PREVIOUS PAGE
*Kenwood, the south front.*
PREVIOUS PAGE *Detail of the decoration on the south front, from Adam's* Works *(1774).*

*The earliest known view of Kenwood, in the background of T. Ramsey's* Heath House, Hampstead, *1755. (Private Collection)*

# THE ORIGINAL HOUSE

John Bill, the King's Printer, probably built the original house shortly after 1616. His choice of site was partly prompted by the fine prospects south towards London, and the clean air. The present brick house may be the work of William Bridges, Surveyor General of the Ordnance, who owned Kenwood from 1694 to 1704. In 1713 he advised his cousin James Bridges, first Duke of Chandos on the building of his seat Cannons, near Edgware. The brick 'double pile' house consists of two horizontal ranges, side by side, a design typical of the late seventeenth century. It appears to have survived without additions until the employment of the Adam brothers from 1764.

No visual record is yet known of the original Jacobean house, but the earliest known images of Kenwood do show the south front before Adam's modifications. Even allowing for artistic licence, these views indicate that the brick house had been covered in stucco and made to resemble a more substantial stone mansion before Adam's arrival. The strict symmetry, the steeply pitched roof and dormer windows suggest that a 'Queen Anne' house lies masked within. The fenestration was presumably mirrored on the unrecorded north front.

# ROBERT AND JAMES ADAM

The importance of Kenwood to the Adam brothers is evident from their lavish *Works in Architecture*; the second part (published in 1774) is devoted solely to the house. Volume I comprised Syon House, Kenwood and Luton Hoo, followed by public buildings and royal commissions. The second volume, published in 1779, covered three London town houses, a continuation of the designs for Syon House, and a miscellany of lesser commissions ranging from a church to a coffee house. Volume III, published posthumously in 1822, contained further designs for Syon House and Luton Hoo, together with engravings relating to work at Edinburgh University, the Adelphi (formerly beside the Thames at Charing Cross), and the three town houses presented in volume II. A promise to publish further engravings of Kenwood, made in volume I, was never kept. This survey of the brothers' commissions was a sophisticated publicity exercise, in which many of the great 'Adam' houses for which they are best known today (such as Harewood, Kedleston, Croome Court, Osterley Park and Bowood) do not feature.

Clearly then, the Adam brothers regarded Kenwood as one of their major commissions, and were sufficiently proud of their achievements to include it among only three houses outside central London included in the *Works*. Significantly, while Syon House and Luton Hoo (then known as 'Luton Park') are described as 'seats', Kenwood is 'the Villa of Earl Mansfield'. This was no country house, set in the heart of a vast agricultural estate, but a rural retreat from the cares of London life. This important distinction was not lost on Robert and his younger brother James when presenting their designs to the Lord Chief Justice, either at Kenwood or in his town house in Bloomsbury Square.

### Robert Adam's 'revolution'

Lord Mansfield had been living at Kenwood for nearly a decade before he turned to the Adam brothers for the architectural remodelling of the house in 1764, probably on the advice of its previous owner, Lord Bute. His choice of the fashionable fellow Scots cannot have been difficult. The Adam brothers had been working at various great houses since Robert's return from Italy in 1758. James Adam toured Italy from 1760 to 1763 and the following year, when the earliest known designs for Kenwood appeared, the brothers were approaching their peak. In 1761 Robert Adam had been appointed joint Architect of the King's Works (partly

through the influence of his fellow countryman Lord Bute, the prime minister) and in 1764 he published the results of his investigations in Dalmatia, *Ruins of the Palace of the Emperor Diocletian at Spalatro*. This publication revealed to many for the first time the domestic architecture of classical times, in contrast to the public buildings on which the influential Palladian style was largely based. Adam's work presented a fresh vocabulary of decorative motifs as an alternative to the formulae recorded by Vitruvius and revived by Palladio and his British admirers. To these motifs Adam was to add elements from sixteenth-century Italian decoration and from contemporary French fashions, whilst adopting many features of the British Palladian movement. His only real rivals at this time were Sir William Chambers (fellow Architect of the King's Works) and James 'Athenian' Stuart.

In the preface to the first volume of their *Works*, the brothers claimed (with some exaggeration in 1773) 'to have brought about . . . a kind of revolution in the whole system of English architecture'. Key principles discussed in the work included the release of architectural ornament from the classical vocabulary prescribed by Vitruvius and Palladio and the creation of overall unity. In their pursuit of 'movement' the Adam brothers revealed their admiration for the 'picturesque'. This fashionable aesthetic theory is most often associated with landscape gardening, and the remodelling of estates to resemble paintings by Claude or Poussin. In architecture the brothers sought a sense of 'movement'. By this, they intended 'the rise and fall, the advance and recess with other diversity of form, in the different parts of a building, so as to add greatly to the picturesque of the composition'. The brothers' application of theories of the picturesque is particularly evident at Kenwood, both indoors and out.

## The remodelling of Kenwood

To whom should the remodelling of Kenwood be attributed? The text in the Kenwood section of the *Works* clearly states that the 'Plans, elevations, and sections of Kenwood' were engraved 'after the Designs of Robert Adam'. However, the initial contribution of James is evident from several designs signed and dated 'James Adam, Archt., 1764'. These were soon superseded by Robert Adam's own proposals. According to Robert Adam, Lord Mansfield 'gave full scope to my ideas: nor were they confined by any circumstances, but the necessity of preserving the proper exterior similitude between the new and the old parts of the buildings; and even with respect to this, where the latter appeared defective in its detail, I was at full liberty to make the proper deviations.' Robert Adam's emphatic statement leaves us

in no doubt that the creative freedom he enjoyed at Kenwood was exceptional, and that the ideas realised here were to be regarded as the fruits of his genius alone, and not of any collaboration with his younger brother or his patron.

Adam's reference to 'the proper exterior similitude between the new and the old parts of the building' reminds us of the amount of architectural remodelling he undertook, rather than designing buildings from the ground up. The building 'boom' of the previous generation, largely in the Palladian style, accounted for most of the great country houses of the eighteenth century. At Syon, Osterley and Kenwood, Adam was employed to remodel even earlier buildings.

At Kenwood, the exterior work extended well beyond any simple addition of a grand porch. The two principal facades present the first full expression of the ambitions Adam had previously realised indoors. Adam's obsession with continuity in design was fully realised for the first time here, both outside and within. Consequently the house is wholly characteristic of the 'Adam style' that was to become so influential. This creative freedom, and its fulfilment, largely accounts for the emphasis given to Kenwood in the *Works*.

In identifying his own work at Kenwood, Robert Adam is quite specific: 'the portico to the north, the great room or library, and its anti-room, are the new additions. . . . The decoration of the south front, excepting that of the west wing, is entirely new, and became in some measure necessary, to conceal the brick-work, which being built at different times, was of various colours – The Attic story is a late addition to the house.'

He also points out, tantalisingly: 'But as many alterations were made, and many inside decorations added, in the apartments of the old house, these are reserved as the subject of another number.' Although no other engravings of Kenwood were published by Adam, numerous designs survive in Sir John Soane's Museum. Together with craftsmen's invoices, these enable us to identify Adam's remarkable remodelling of the interior. His versatility, whether designing porticos or door knobs, chimneypieces or chairs, resulted in a consistency in design and overall sense of unity. At Kenwood he developed his principles of harmony through geometry, colour and repetition of motifs with a fascination for detail well beyond the patience of the great architect-designer of the Palladian era, William Kent. This aspect of Adam's work at Kenwood is discussed more fully in chapter 1.

Designs of Kenwood, *the unused design, dated 1773, for the title page of Robert and James Adam's* Works *part II. (By courtesy of the Trustees of Sir John Soane's Museum)*

Robert Adam *by James Tassie. The most ambitious of the four sons of William Adam, a leading Scottish architect, Robert Adam (1728–92) created his own distinct style of architecture and interior design, drawing upon influences as varied as classical antiquity, sixteenth-century Italian decoration, theories of the picturesque, and contemporary French fashions.*

North Front of Caen Wood, *engraving after Conrad Metz, 1782 showing the house's original setting divided from Hampstead Lane by the 'Great Court' and a high stone wall. Walls within the forecourt concealed the 'Kitchen Garden' to the east and the 'Kitchen Court' to the west.*

# THE NORTH FRONT

The entrance front today is unaltered since Adam's time, but for the addition of two flanking wings by the 2nd Earl of Mansfield between 1793 and 1796, and later repairs. However, the setting is quite different, as is clear from an engraving published in 1782 after Conrad Metz. Until the second Earl created the North Wood, the road linking Hampstead and Highgate passed much closer to the house, approximately where the lawn meets the trees today. The general effect would have been far more imposing than it is today, asserting both the status and character of Kenwood's eminent owner.

*Detail of the portico*

As a result of the second Earl's changes, we now leave Hampstead Lane and descend one of two twisting leafy drives. Suddenly we emerge into a great pool of light and discover the secluded house, seen from an oblique angle. The whole experience is mysterious and dramatic, more befitting the age of Romanticism than the neoclassical taste with which Adam is identified.

## The portico

Adam records in his *Works* that 'The portico to the north is the only part of that front which is new'. However, much of the surface decoration, culminating in corner pilasters (now partially cropped by the brick wings) dates from his time, and conceals the brick building within. The addition of the grand portico, rising the full height of the original two-storey house, distinguished the main residence from several outbuildings scattered within this side of the estate. The portico also gave Kenwood some prominence, for the house, rising above the perimeter wall, could be seen by passers-by on horseback, as a conspicuous yet private residence. The sloping site and lack of a 'rustic' ground storey also made the high portico essential, for they ruled out the possibility of an imposing flight of steps. Since the creation of the North Wood, the descending drives and the two brick wings by the second Earl, the entrance front with its projecting portico has effectively sunk and receded, reducing the sense of grandeur intended by the first Earl and Adam.

The portico is inspired by public architecture of classical times (specifically the Erechtheion on the Athenian Acropolis), in marked contrast to the later south front and interior, where Adam drew more upon his own researches into the domestic architecture of the ancient Greeks and Romans, and on a variety of later sources. However, the portico is elaborately ornamented and the choice of capital for the columns is original, combining characteristics of the Ionic and Corinthian orders.

The preface to the Kenwood part of the *Works* includes a lengthy discussion of the comparative merits of the orders of classical architecture. The proportions and types of columns, capitals and bases were the subject of great controversy 'among modern architects' and Adam took the opportunity to set out his working principles on this issue: 'Architecture has not, like some others arts, an immediate standard in nature ... it must be formed and improved by a correct taste, and diligent study of the beauties exhibited by great masters in their productions.' In considering the five classical orders, he similarly speaks as a creative artist and not as an upholder of academic traditions:

In the first place, we acknowledge only three orders; the Doric, the Ionic, and the Corinthian: for as to the Tuscan, it is, in fact, no more than a bad and imperfect

Doric; and the Composite, or Roman order, in our opinion, is a very disagreeable and awkward mixture of the Corinthian and Ionic, without either grace or beauty. We do not however mean to condemn the composing of capitals; a liberty which has been often taken by the ancients with great success.

Many liberties were taken at Kenwood in the name of taste. An architect of the previous generation would have conceived the portico in the Corinthian order, the most elaborate order and thus traditionally used for the finest buildings. Adam states his preference for Ionic capitals quite clearly in the preface to the Kenwood section of the *Works*: 'The Corinthian capital itself does not, in our opinion, admit of more dignity and magnificence, than a rich Ionic with its volutes square in the front . . .'. He greatly prefers volutes set 'square', as at Kenwood, aligned with the pediment, rather than projecting at an angle from each corner as 'they have been injudiciously adopted by Michael Angelo, Scamozzi, and many other modern architects'. Beyond simply preferring the Ionic order, Adam has a further refinement to recommend:

The great size of the volute of the Grecian Ionic has always appeared to us by much too heavy, and those used by the Romans seem rather to border on the other extreme. We have therefore generally taken a mean between them, which we think has a happy effect. . . . We have also adopted the Grecian manner of forming the volute with a double fillet, which, by producing more light and shade, gives great relief, and far exceeds in grace and beauty that used by the Romans. In imitation of the Greeks, we likewise bend the channel, or hollow band, from whence the volutes spring, in the middle of the capital.

With astonishing self-assurance, Adam recommends such modifications to time-honoured architectural conventions, and like an artist creating an abstract sculpture, he relies ultimately on his own artistic taste. However, this taste is characteristic of his time, for Adam's primary concern for light and shade, weight and relief, and the importance he attaches to the setting of an architectural feature, reveal his fascination with fashionable theories of the picturesque, and their application to architecture.

In stating his preference for Greek over Roman ornament, Adam also entered into the 'battle of the styles' then raging. He did much to postpone this 'battle' until the early years of the nineteenth century, through his highly personal and influential assimilation of different periods and principles into what became known as the 'Adam style'. The portico at Kenwood is, as stated earlier, a quotation from the Erechtheion at Athens. This classical building is more familiar to Londoners today through a closer copy in Euston Road: St Pancras Church of 1819–22, designed by William Inwood (son of the 1st Earl of Mansfield's bailiff at Kenwood) and his elder son, H. W. Inwood.

The earliest known craftsman's account for the exterior of Kenwood was submitted by Joseph Rose and is dated 1768–9. He charged Lord Mansfield for the 'Dorick Cornice in hard Stucco making part of Pedem[t]', together with the 'Frize with Cabled fluting & Pateras' and the 'Medallion with enr[d] frame'. Either he was not paid, or he later resumed work, for Rose submitted another account, dated 1773, for the 'Cornice in Portico Ogee enr[d] with raffled leafe' together with 'Goloss under great beams' (by which he meant the *guilloche* decoration to be seen on the underside of the pediment) and, once again, 'A Medallion of three figures with

*Detail of the portico. Adam's composite capitals crown the fluted columns with the scrolling volutes of the Ionic order, seemingly compressed like giant springs beneath the great weight of the pediment they support. Each capital is divided from the columns by a collar of carved acanthus leaves that seem to sprout from the fluting. Like Corinthian capitals, they echo vegetation.*

*Plan of Kenwood, published in Robert and James Adam's* Works *(1774), showing the original service wing behind the 'Green House' (Orangery).*

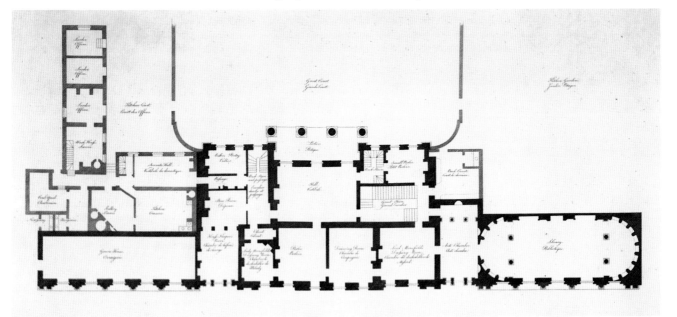

enrich'd frame around'. The bold decoration beneath the pediment is particularly striking.

The accounts of 1773 also include a payment to Eleanor Coade (the manufacturer of 'Coadestone', a twice-fired clay ideally suited to cast ornament) for seventy-eight and a half feet of 'enrich'd facia'. Although 'Caenwood' is included in the list of commissions published in the catalogue to the Coade Gallery in 1799, the actual work is not specified. Precisely where Rose's 'hard Stucco' ends and the Coadestone begins is still uncertain, but the frieze of swags and flower-heads beneath the pediment corresponds with a Coade design, is the appropriate clay colour beneath the paintwork and is still crisp and complete as is typical of Coadestone. The earliest work presumably proved faulty. Rose's work in 'hard stucco' beneath the portico owes its preservation to being protected from the weather. A new 'Mahogany glass door' was also fitted in 1773.

The north front of Kenwood must have been admired from further afield, for in 1779 Adam's engraving of this facade was re-published in Leipzig as an illustration to *Théorie de l'Art des Jardins* by Christian Hirschfeld.

# THE NORTH WINGS

The two wings on the north front were added by the 2nd Earl of Mansfield between 1793 (when he inherited Kenwood and the family title) and his death in 1796. It is tempting to speculate whether Robert Adam would have returned to work at Kenwood, had he lived. Robert Adam died on 3 March 1792, and as Viscount Stormont, the future earl had been one of the pall-bearers at the architect's funeral in Westminster Abbey. At his sudden death from a stomach haemorrhage Adam had twenty-five private commissions and eight public buildings still in hand, and numbered Lord Stormont among his past patrons. James Adam died in October 1794, after submitting an estimate to the second Earl for repairs to his town house the previous year (see below).

### George Saunders, architect
Robert Nasmith was the second Earl's rather obscure first choice as his architect, but he in turn died, on 30 August 1793. His place was taken by George Saunders (c.1762–1839), who was already employed as surveyor at Kenwood. Saunders was not the first choice of Humphry Repton, the landscape gardener, whose advice on both buildings and grounds the second Earl had already sought. Repton took credit for advising Nasmith, and recommended the architect William Wilkins the elder as his successor:

as your Lordship did me the honour to adopt many of the hints with which I furnished him for Kenwood, it would be desirable if I were in the same way to communicate my ideas to his successor in the management of your Lordships buildings . . . that our operations both within without doors may harmonise with each other.

At thirty-one Saunders was five years younger than Robert Adam had been when his family firm began their designs for Kenwood. However, Saunders proved to be far less promising and he still remains little-known today. Presumably the second Earl did not wish to outshine Adam's achievement at Kenwood by employing a more eminent architect.

Saunders seems to have specialised in extensions in earlier styles. He already held the post of Surveyor to the Trustees of the British Museum since 1792, and from 1801–03 he designed a Palladian extension to its premises in Montague House, Bloomsbury. After the 2nd Earl of Mansfield's death in 1796 he was employed by the third Earl to remodel the family's Scottish seat, Scone Palace, in a Georgian Jacobean style. His designs were never executed and he was succeeded there by the architect William Atkinson, who also undertook extensive repairs at Kenwood in 1815–17 (see chapter 3). Saunders' work at Kenwood is in the spirit of Adam, but his interior decoration reveals the influence of Henry Holland, particularly the latter's fashionable modifications of Carlton House, Pall Mall (demolished in 1828) for George, Prince of Wales.

### Additions and embellishments
The 'Stone Wing' to the right as you face the portico contains the Dining Room on the ground floor, corresponding with the Music Room in the so-called 'Pink Wing' opposite. The first floors of both contained additional bedrooms. Linked by Adam's entrance hall, the wings provided a new suite of reception rooms, one of which included the first permanent dining room at Kenwood. Such additions must have seemed essential to the retired British Ambassador to Vienna and, subsequently, to Paris.

The new Earl acted so swiftly following the death of his uncle at Kenwood on 18 March 1793 that we may assume he had long awaited this opportunity to enlarge the villa and transform it into a family seat. In June 1793 the first account was submitted for 'Removing of Ground to prepare for the Foundations of the New Offices'. This would have been for the Service Wing, concealed from view from the entrance front by the Dining Room wing (see below). On 27 July 1793 a payment was made to 'Mr. J. Saunders for his plans'. The first payment for the diversion of Hampstead Lane away from the end of the original forecourt to its present position (beyond

the screening North Wood) was made to John Dearmer on 17 August 1793. On 29 August 1793 the second Earl wrote from West Cowes to Sir William Hamilton:

I am here with my whole family. . . . In less than a fortnight we shall return to Kenwood where I am carrying on very extensive works. Offices were absolutely necessary, and as Lord Mansfield had so frequently recommended to me the embellishment of Kenwood I resolved that they should be upon a handsome plan. This draws on an addition to the house etc. I had naturally an aversion to Brick and Mortar, but I doubt I am engaged now for life. The improvements out of doors I shall delight in, as that is a subject, which in a degree at least I understand.

The improvements, prompted by the first Earl, did not pass unnoticed. On 21 November 1793 the artist Joseph Farington noted in his diary:

A very fine day for the season. After breakfast I rode out, and passed through Highgate, by Caen wood, to Hampstead. The ride at a moderate rate in an hour and a half. Lord Stormont is making considerable & in respect of architectural effect strange additions to the late Lord Mansfields house at Caen wood.

The two wings on the north front did not feature among such 'strange additions' for the accounts include under 19 July 1794: 'Give the Bricklayers by Lady Caroline who laid the first Brick of the North Wing . . . 1. 1. 6'. Lady Caroline Murray was the second Earl's daughter. In 1794 work began on the octagonal farm building, designed by William Marshall; new stables were built the following year.

The plain design of the two wings has long been regarded as an example of the reaction against Adam in fashionable taste that occurred towards the end of the eighteenth century. Compared to the handsome entrance facade, the wings are almost austere. Adam says he encased the earlier red and brown house in white cement, thereby concealing the variety of colours of brick, and suggesting a house built of stone. The second Earl's choice of white Suffolk bricks (briefly made fashionable by Henry Holland) reduced the need for such embellishment. The bricks

*The north front today, with the white brick wings added by the 2nd Earl of Mansfield and his architect George Saunders, 1793–6.*

*Decoration on the south front, as engraved for Robert and James Adam's* Works *(1774).*

were left plain without any continuation of Adam's fluted frieze and string-course from the entrance facade. The cornice, featuring a dentelled (tooth-like) frieze above an egg and dart moulding, runs around the roof line, and a stone skirting continues from the entrance facade. No attempt was made to mask the abrupt collision between the new brick wings and the pilasters which had elegantly framed the original composition.

A note among the second Earl's accounts reveals that this contrast resulted not so much from the fashionable reaction against Adam's love of ornament, but rather from the second Earl's desire that Adam's original work should not be confused with later additions. On 6 August 1793 he noted for himself:

Points that must ultimately [be] decided tomorrow and the decision put down in writing to prevent the possibility of mistake.
   Elevation of the Dining Room. I shall be inclind to prefer that which has the least ornament as it must be self evident that these projecting wings were not built at the same time with the Body of the House, and as that Body is far from being regular, it is my opinion that the wings should be so built as to appear chaste simple buildings in themselves.

His resolution not to cover the wings in any form of cement also had a practical motive, one which must have been underlined weeks later when he received James Adam's 'Estimate for repairing the composition at the back of the Earl of Mansfield's House in Portland Place', dated 29 August 1793. Below the total price of £266.18.3½ the second Earl wrote 'cannot agree to have the stucco repaired as the expense would be so great'. So ended the historic association between the Mansfield and Adam families.

# THE GARDEN FRONT

In the Music Room wing, symmetry is preserved by the use of blind windows facing the Dining Room wing (only one of the six windows in the facade is real). Inside the Music Room, behind the further blind window at the northern end of

the wing, stood the chamber organ. Continuing around to the garden front of this wing we cross the line of the previous forecourt wall. A copper-roofed veranda links the Music Room wing to the back of the pre-Adam Orangery. The cast-iron columns are clearly inspired by the balustrade on Adam's grand staircase within, while the Ionic capitals echo the portico.

The large, full-length windows remind us that the Music Room also served as a drawing room, facing west towards the afternoon sunlight across a lawn filled with crescent-shaped flowerbeds. This garden was created by the second and third Earls on the site of the previous service wing; it provided a more intimate and colourful outlook than the sweeping prospect south towards London that inspired Adam in designing the Library. This was a change in outlook in both senses. Before the trees grew to their present height the vista was crowned by the dairy cottages, intended to resemble a group of Swiss chalets. The ivy arbour is a characteristic feature of Repton's landscape designs. Like the second Earl's serpentine drives which enhance our sense of discovering the north front, this small leafy tunnel suddenly opens on to the great natural amphitheatre of the south lawns and ponds. The effect is unforgettable.

# THE SOUTH FRONT

Adam was sufficiently proud of the south front of Kenwood to make it the subject of his only perspective view of the house (see page 53). In addition, the south front featured as one of two 'geometrical elevations' in the *Works*, while a further engraving was devoted to details of the decoration. In the accompanying text Adam twice points out the novelty of his treatment of this facade whilst explaining how he was inspired by Kenwood's remarkable setting:

The whole scene is amazingly gay, magnificent, beautiful, and picturesque. The hill and dale are finely diversified; nor is it easy to imagine a situation more striking without, or more agreeably retired and peaceful within. The decoration bestowed on this front of the house is suitable to such a scene. The idea is new, and has been generally approved. . . . The decoration of

*The initial design for the south front, c.1764.*

the south front, excepting that of the west wing, is entirely new and became in some measure necessary, to conceal the brick-work, which being built at different times, was of various colours.

Adam created symmetry (so loved by architects in this neoclassical era) by building the Library wing to balance with the earlier Orangery and then refacing the whole composition in a patent cement. He may have heeded the warning of Isaac Ware, who in his *Complete Body of Architecture* (1768) observed: 'We see an addition of a great room now to almost every house of consequence ... in those houses which are ridiculous for their new rooms, the addition is made without any regard to the whole fabrick.'

In the *Works* Adam also advertised his ingenuity in making a further addition to the south range of the house. He took advantage of the sloping site to add a third storey on the south side without any conspicuous difference between the height of the north and south roofs. As he informed his readers: 'The Attic story is a late addition to the house, and was executed in a singular manner, the walls being raised, and the new roof covered in, before the old one was removed and thus was the house left habitable, and unexposed to the injuries of the weather, during the whole progress of this useful alteration.'

### Decoration of the south front

The general character of the south front is in marked contrast to the entrance facade, and derives more from Adam's experiments with interior decoration than from classical and Palladian precedents. Unlike the massive columns and heavy projecting pediment of the north front, creating bold contrasts in light and shade, we find an essay in low relief, in linear patterns without any reference to the construction within. Similar decoration can be found in the library at Kenwood, and is characteristic of Adam's increasing tendency towards detail and refinement. It effectively defines the terrace as a domestic space, an extension of the interior, in contrast to the entrance facade.

Reactions to this novel treatment were mixed. Early interest is revealed by the first engraving of Kenwood, published in *A New*

*Display of the Beauties of England* at least a year before the Kenwood section of Adam's *Works* appeared. In 1781 *The Morning Herald* devoted an article to Kenwood, and began with this facade, noting 'its condition and appearance are, alone, sufficient to establish its pretensions to public favours'. However, two years before, Robert Smirke (father of the architect) published a pamphlet attacking Adam, in particular his treatment of facades. Smirke complained: 'While he aimed at elegance within, he covered the outside of his buildings with frippery.' To his mind 'Most of the white walls, with which Mr Adam has speckled this city, are no better than Models for the Twelfth-Night Decoration of a Pastry Cook.'

Certainly, many visitors today find the South Front at Kenwood more akin to a wedding cake than a great house. Much of the decoration is lost when seen from afar and it seems more suitable for a street facade. We must assume that it was intended for family and guests parading along the terrace and seeing it from close-to, at an oblique angle, preferably in a raking early afternoon light.

The earliest-known design, dated 1764, gives no indication of this remarkable development in British architecture (see opposite). The finished office drawing, clearly made before the proposal to add the attic storey, either mirrored the north front or was later transferred to the opposite facade, for the central block is almost identical, but for the use of Corinthian rather than Ionic capitals. The Library windows were to be as large as those to the Orangery; the two Venetian windows in the link buildings do not appear to include the doors that were built.

In the later design, dated 1767–8 (see below), the portico is reduced to paired pilasters and a pediment in shallow relief, raised above a ground storey 'rusticated' to resemble cut stone. The three levels are identified in the engraving of the decoration as the 'Attic', the 'Bed Chamber Story' and the 'Basement'. The sudden contrasts, between the plain Basement flanked by the columns of the Orangery and Library wings, and the variety of the two storeys above, reminds us of Adam's love of 'movement' in architecture and of the delight he took in using it to manipulate the emotions of his patrons' families and guests.

*Detail of the Library decoration, as engraved for the* Works *(1774).*

*The south front, as engraved for the* Works *(1774).*

*The linear patterns on the south front are an extension of Adam's decoration in the Library and help to define the terrace as a domestic space in contrast to the entrance facade. Adam emphasised in the* Works *(1774) that the idea of using such ornament outside was new. However, the experiment proved only partly successful, as the decoration soon crumbled and perished.*

The contrast between the two facades may have various explanations other than the development of Robert Adam's style beyond the less imaginative approach of his brother. Whereas the north front is grand and imposing, making a sober impression on visitors as we arrive and enter Lord Mansfield's hall, here on the south front the effect is less formal. We have passed through the reception suite and can relax. Our eyes are invited to linger and explore a great orchestra of motifs, rooted in the classical tradition but modified and combined with an artist's originality and wit. This contrast had its parallel in the public and private character of Lord Mansfield. Essentially, however, the revised south front was a result of Adam's response to the prospect his facade faces, the inspiring setting he found 'magnificent, beautiful, and picturesque'.

## Liardet's oil cement

Craftsmen's accounts reveal that Joseph Rose completed the south front in 1773, but that repairs had to be made by 1781. Rose may have encountered difficulties with the cement for his account, dated 15 May 1773, specifies 'To painting & making good the Artificial stone fascia & to other parts of the front'. Completion is indicated by an account of 29 May 1773 for 'making good the finishing in the south front'. However, an account from 1778 includes 'To Cutting down the old plaister of the front of Miss Murray's Room and of the Green House'. The Orangery (as it is now known) was then covered

'in Liardet'. Three years later a fuller account 'For Liardet Composition executed at his Lordships Seat at Kenwood' by John Raffields includes a 'deduction of £20 on account of the loss sustained by the late repairs' signed by Robert Adam.

'Liardet' was an oil cement named after its inventor, a Swiss clergyman who patented it in 1773. It promised a cheap means of reproducing architectural decoration. The Adam brothers purchased his patent and then another from the less colourfully named Mr Wark, who had invented the material Liardet improved. In a further attempt to monopolise the new material, the firm even obtained an Act of Parliament (when Robert Adam was an MP) giving them the exclusive right to manufacture 'Adam's new invented patent stucco'. In 1778 they prosecuted a Mr Johnson who had obtained a patent for his own improved stucco. The case came before Lord Mansfield, who found in the brothers' favour, and accusations of partiality fuelled the increasing criticism of the firm, prompting pamphlets. They were ahead of the fashion for white stucco facades, which is more identified with Wyatt, Nash and the Regency period. But they were still architects of their time; 'Liardet' is a vivid example of their fascination in the 1770s with new manufactured materials produced by the Industrial Revolution.

The south front of Kenwood would have been a great advertisement for this material, and the three engravings published in the *Works* in 1774 would have encouraged potential clients to view

the house. The press certainly responded. For example, as early as 16 October 1775 the *Morning Chronicle* reported that Kenwood was 'beautifully new fronted with terras invented by the Messrs. Adams; and it is imagined from its durability, that most new houses will be finished with it'. The article on Kenwood in the *Morning Herald* on 21 September 1781 could have been contrived to answer the critics' pamphlets, for the opening comment on the south front makes no mention of its recent repair, but notes 'The composition is now, after an exposure of seven years, unspotted; it has not in any part lost its adhesion, and has visibly increased in whiteness, with increasing age'. Lord Mansfield would not have agreed. According to Humphry Repton 'The great Lord Mansfield often declared, that had the front of Kenwood been originally covered in Parian marble, he should have found it less expensive than stucco.' The decoration continued to deteriorate and the facade was long left plain. The details we see today were recreated in fibreglass from Adam's engravings by the Greater London Council in 1975.

The perspective view of the south front published in the Adams' *Works* clearly shows a small pavilion closing the terrace to the east (see above). It might be considered as unreal as the young maidens in classical dress who run past the eighteenth-century gentlemen and dog in the engraving, were it not for the survival of a finished scaled drawing in Sir John Soane's Museum, dated 1771, and the discovery of a line of bricks at right angles to the house during the

repair of a burst water main in 1974. The drawing reveals that it was intended to have a bay window facing east, and an elaborately decorated ceiling. If built, the pavilion would have helped to block the view from the public path that linked Hampstead Lane and Millfield Lane in the first Earl's time.

In the same engraving a short wall runs east along the terrace from the end of the Library. This survives and contains a door opening on to steps leading down to the Service Wing. The present ground level of this rear courtyard dates only from the creation of the Service Wing in 1793–7. A further modern flight of steps descends to the original ground level and the entrance to the Cold Bath.

# THE COLD BATH

The 'Cold Bath' probably dates from the early eighteenth century, when cold bathing was most fashionable. It appears in Robert Adam's original plans of Kenwood, but not in the overlay containing his proposals. The rectangular bath with steps in one corner recorded at that time was later remodelled, when the oval walls with niches were also created. The exterior plan remains unchanged. The bath is supplied by a nearby spring, several of which may be found on the Kenwood estate and on Hampstead Heath. Indeed, Hampstead largely developed as a spa and resort town in the eighteenth century on the strength of its mineral springs.

Cold bathing was popular for medicinal reasons, rather than for personal cleanliness. The cold or tepid water must have been highly invigorating for some, and unpleasant for others who took the plunge in search of its presumed therapeutic powers. One of bathing's many advocates, the doctor Sir John Floyer, believed such bathing could help to cure rickets, rabies, leprosy, impotence, and much more, and recommended 'you must use the cold Bath at 11 or 12 in the Morning, and not when very hot; not at Night'. The popularity of other spa towns, particularly Bath, and abroad at Spa and Baden, prompted the gentry to build their own cold baths on their return from such resorts. Consequently cold baths can be found at several gentlemen's seats, some indoors and some within picturesque garden pavilions. At Kedleston, for example, the cold bath Adam designed in 1769, set within a boat house and below a fishing room, still stands.

The earliest reference to Kenwood's cold bath, in an account for 'Labour in & about the Cold Bath' in 1762, suggests that the 1st Earl of Mansfield had an earlier bath substantially restored for his use. Repairs to the drain, pipes and surrounding fence and rail were also carried out at the end of his life, between 1791 and 1793.

The bath we see today has only recently been fully restored following excavation. The lining in Carrara statuary marble, the surrounding walkway, steps and the domed vault are all reconstruction. Evidence of the original marble floor was only found after excavating through a later floor of Purbeck limestone and some three feet of silt and rubble, until a layer of purple slates and terracotta tiles was reached. This waterproof lining bore traces of mortar in which fragments of white marble were embedded, including the octagonal black band here recreated. Clearly, the original marble lining had been removed and the bath itself allowed to silt up in the nineteenth century until rubble and a later floor were added. The window sills were then raised and new windows inserted. The use of Portland cement in these later alterations suggests a date after 1820. Presumably it then became a garden store.

Excavation also revealed evidence of the original decoration of the walls. Over twenty oyster shells remained, affixed to the plaster walls. Statues may have stood in the niches and on the plinth facing the door. A row of hooks found on the rear wall may have held a curtain or tapestry and further brackets lower down suggest the presence of decorated plasterwork, again facing the entrance. A considerable imaginative leap is necessary before we may picture Lord or Lady Mansfield gingerly stepping into this precursor of the jacuzzi.

# THE SERVICE WING

Behind the row of white Doric columns opposite the Cold Bath stands the substantial Service Wing built by George Saunders for the 2nd Earl of Mansfield between 1793 and 1796, and completed by Saunders in 1797 for the third Earl.

The previous service wing, known to the first Earl and the Adam brothers, stood behind the Orangery. It must have been both inadequate for the second Earl's needs and an obstruction. Demolition allowed space for a new garden, provided light for the new Music Room, and opened up the view west from this room towards the afternoon sun. Removal of the servants' quarters and kitchens to the east side made them far less noticeable in the second Earl's scheme.

The new Service Wing was built of rare purple-brown London stocks, in deliberate contrast to the white bricks used by Saunders for the additions to the main house. It was clearly intended to be as inconspicuous as possible, and the embankment of the terrace helped both to conceal the building from the pleasure garden, and to block the servants' view of their masters at leisure.

Together with the adjacent cellars beneath the Adam Library and north wing the Service Wing contains a warren of over sixty rooms. These include beer and wine cellars (one still contains two giant casks evidently created where they still stand), servants' quarters, a wash house, pantry, and all other rooms necessary to the daily running of a gentleman's family seat, rather than the smaller villa frequented by the first Earl. The earliest dated plan of the wing, from 1815, includes thirteen bedrooms for staff, some large enough for several servants. A further indication of the scale of life at Kenwood in the third Earl's time is given by a 'List of wines in Kenwood cellars', drawn up on 21 March 1840, shortly after the third Earl's death. The following is only an extract:

Botles Port Wine   1315
Botles Sherry   921
Botles Champagne   122
Botles Cherry Brandy   14
1120   Gallons of Ale
250   Gallons of Small Beer.

## The Old Kitchen
The largest room is the vast kitchen, which originally rose the full height of the Service Wing. It is entered through the loggia of columns opposite the Cold Bath. This is now the Kenwood restaurant, with the cafeteria occupying the old laundry and brew house alongside. These are the only rooms open to the public at present, but further restoration is in progress to reveal Kenwood's 'life below stairs'.

The splayed corners make the square room octagonal, a shape suggested to Saunders by Humphry Repton, the landscape gardener, while he was preparing designs for Lord Mansfield. Repton had in mind the medieval Abbot's Kitchen at Glastonbury. The blocked windows at each corner remain a mystery. Old photographs of the kitchen reveal that the two dressers originally stood in opposite positions, with a doorway from the scullery in the centre of the wall facing the fireplace. The present entrance from the trellis avenue, with its fanlight above, dates from 1954. Along the wall facing the present entrance runs the old range of charcoal hotplates, over which a hood was originally suspended; this would have directed smoke and cooking smells up the sloping walls within the recesses and so out through the windows.

The kitchen grate, spit and adjacent ranges of baking ovens and warming cupboards were manufactured by the ironmongers Johnson & Ravey, who traded under this name at the address shown on the spit mechanism between 1847 and 1910. The Kenwood inventory of 1831 itemises every piece of equipment in the Kitchen. For example, the long list of 'Coppers' includes '43 stew pans & covers 35 fluted pudding moulds'. The large collection of copperware or 'batterie de cuisine' now at Scone Palace includes pieces bearing Johnson & Ravey's stamp which probably came from Kenwood. Some of the highly important eighteenth-century porcelain at Scone is also included in the 1831 inventory; it was discovered in cupboards in the Service Wing at Kenwood shortly before the house auction of 1922.

To reach the second Earl's dining table from this kitchen food had to travel along the corridor behind the open colonnade and into the basement of the Dining Room wing. Here a stone staircase led up to the Dining Room lobby (see Chapter 1). Communication over such distances was only possible from the end of the eighteenth century after the development of the bell-pull into elaborate systems employing wires and cranks.

The gate lodges, stables and new farm built for the second Earl are not, as yet, open to the public. However, a short walk downhill from the Service Wing to the 'Thousand Pound Pond' will reveal the true nature of Kenwood's only bogus architectural feature, the 'sham bridge' (see chapter 5), as well as providing a classic view of the south front.

*The Service Wing, built by George Saunders between 1793 and 1797 for the 2nd and 3rd Earls of Mansfield.*

## Chapter Three
# RESIDENTS, VISITORS AND GUESTS

Throughout the recorded history of Kenwood one consistent characteristic unites the successive residents: their dependence upon London. Kenwood is not a 'country house' or a 'stately home' in the sense of a self-sufficient ancestral seat set in the heart of a great agricultural estate, but rather a villa, a suburban retreat from the cares of the capital, in which residents and their guests would relax, study and entertain.

To some extent the Kenwood estate has reflected the changing centres of wealth and power in this country, through the variety of its owners. These include a priory, King Henry VIII, and King Charles I's printer. From 1712 Kenwood was owned by a succession of Scotsmen, including the prime minister John Stuart, 3rd Earl of Bute and, from 1754, the Lord Chief Justice, William Murray, 1st Earl of Mansfield. Kenwood remained in the Mansfield family until 1925, when, after the villa had been leased first to a Russian Grand Duke, and then to an American millionairess, it was purchased by an Irishman, Edward Cecil Guinness, 1st Earl of Iveagh. The reason for this Scottish connection (which extended to the architects Robert and James Adam) is not obvious, and it may seem ironic that the very 'Englishness' of Kenwood today results from the patronage and aspirations of the Scots and Irish.

Lord Iveagh did not live at Kenwood, and among the past residents the 1st Earl of Mansfield takes precedence. His professional achievements and his patronage of Robert Adam, his brother and their craftsmen, made Kenwood famous, prompting engravings and articles, and attracting a variety of visitors. Many were drawn by the cult that grew up around Mansfield, making the house and its great library almost a shrine to the great lawyer. Today the furnishings have changed and for many visitors any homage to Mansfield is overshadowed by the character of Rembrandt, through the artist's unforgettable self-portrait.

A View from Caenwood
House over London *by John
Wootton, 1755. Detail, showing
Lord Mansfield, his nieces with
their black companion, and the
artist (Private Collection).*
PREVIOUS PAGE Caen Wood
*by James Heath, 1793 (detail)*

# EARLY OWNERS OF THE ESTATE

The earliest identified owner of the estate,
William de Blemont, came from a prominent city
family with large estates to which they gave the
name Blemundsbury (Bloomsbury). On
becoming a canon in 1226 he granted his forests
between Kentish Town and the Bishop of
London's estate, Hornsey Park, to the Priory of
Holy Trinity, Aldgate. Kenwood then remained
in monastic ownership for three centuries until
the Priory was dissolved in 1532 by Henry VIII.
The King initially exchanged it for Copped Hall
Park, owned by the monastery of Waltham Holy
Cross, until he dissolved the latter in 1540.
Leaseholders developed the commercial
potential of these remains of the ancient Forest of
Middlesex, felling timber and grazing horses and
cattle on cleared land, as did freeholders to a
lesser extent after 1565 when 'Cane Woode'
passed from the Crown to a succession of private
owners.

For the greater part of the seventeenth
century Kenwood belonged to the Bill family of
printers. In 1616 the estate was sold to John Bill
who had risen from being a stationer's
apprentice to become the King's Printer after
1620. Bill built the first house, which his son
inherited in 1630. The younger John Bill, also
King's Printer, fought in the Civil War; his estate
was confiscated until he recognised Parliament,
but he was later fined for his continued efforts in
the Royalist cause. In 1690 his son Charles Bill
sold the estate to Brook Bridges, and by 1694 it
belonged to William Bridges, Surveyor-General
of the Ordnance at the Tower of London. In
1704 he sold Kenwood to a London merchant,
John Walter, who, in 1711, sold it to William,
4th Earl of Berkeley.

In 1616 the estate covered some 460 acres,
but by 1711 it had shrunk to just 'Cane Wood
House, with four ponds containing 2 acres, and
land adjoining the kitchen garden containing 2
acres, and woodland in Panckeridge or St.
Pancras containing 22 acres ... with four other
ponds'. In 1712 Lord Berkeley wrote to Thomas
Wentworth, Earl of Strafford: 'You cannot image
how I enjoy myself at Cane Wood ... and how
quiet and pleasant it is.' But a few days later he
wrote again:

Your Lordship will wonder to hear I have sold Cane
Wood. A Lord Blantyre of Scotland offer'd me 4000
pounds for it, which I thought worth hearkening to,
considering the little time I stay out of town, and that a
place of half that sum might serve me. I wish I may get
a house in your neighbourhood of Twitnam, for I was
always fond of that part of the country. I am still at
Cane Wood, but would be glad to remove since it is
none of my own. It seems 'tis the D. of Argyle hath
bought it under another name ...

So began the ownership of Kenwood by Scottish
aristocrats that continued until 1925. For some
Scots, the wild and hilly countryside of the Heath
may have appealed more than fashionable
Twickenham and Richmond as it evoked
memories of their homeland, rather than of
Venice and the Brenta Canal. As Lady
Stormont, wife of the 1st Earl of Mansfield's
nephew, wrote from Kenwood in 1776: 'There is
something in the noise of the wind and quietness,
and altogether not being used ever to be in the
country in England, I cannot persuade myself I
am not in Scotland.'

After the Act of Union of 1707 many Scots
came to London to seek preferment at Court and
then purchased English estates. This bid for
social acceptance contributed to the
development of Kenwood. However, the fear of
Jacobitism, particularly after the failed uprisings
of 1715 and 1745, fuelled prejudice against the
Scots; in 1780 it nearly brought about
Kenwood's destruction, when anti-Jacobite
feelings mixed with opposition to Catholic
emancipation inflamed the spirit of the Gordon
Rioters who marched on the home of the Lord
Chief Justice.

In 1715, three years after acquiring
Kenwood from Lord Berkeley, John Campbell,
2nd Duke of Argyll conveyed the house and
estate to his brother, Archibald Campbell, Earl
of Ilay, and to his brother-in-law James Stuart,
2nd Earl of Bute. Ilay became Lord Justice
General for Scotland in 1710 and was later
entrusted with all Scottish affairs by the King's
first minister, Robert Walpole. In 1720 Ilay and
Bute sold Kenwood to William Dale, an
upholsterer of Covent Garden who had made a
fortune by investing in the 'South Sea Bubble'
before it burst. But five months later he
mortgaged the property back to Ilay to raise
funds and in 1725 Ilay reclaimed the estate, Dale
having failed to pay back his debt. It appears
that Kenwood was then rented by George
Middleton, an early partner in Coutts Bank,
from 1725 until his death in 1747.

# JOHN STUART, 3rd EARL OF BUTE (1713–92)

Ilay conveyed his half share of Kenwood to his
nephew, John Stuart, 3rd Earl of Bute, in 1746.
Bute is best known as tutor to the future
George III and subsequently (from 1762 until
his resignation the following year) the most
unpopular prime minister this country has
known. Bute's enemies resented his influence
over the King, and accused him of appointing

Archibald Campbell, Earl of
Ilay and later 3rd Duke of
Argyll, *by William Aikman,
c.1715. (Reproduced by gracious
permission of Her Majesty the
Queen)*

fellow Scots to positions vacated by Whigs.

Bute had inherited his father's half-share in the Kenwood estate when he was just ten years old. On the advice of his uncle, Lord Ilay, he had left Scotland for England in 1746 to secure a larger income for his family and in 1750 Bute became Lord of the Bedchamber to Frederick Prince of Wales. He only fully entered into politics after leaving Kenwood in 1754, but during his time here he repaired, redecorated and furnished the house, planted 'exotics' between the house and the south wood, fathered five children, and measured the rainfall.

Bute's enthusiasm for Kenwood, particularly the grounds and situation, is clear from a letter he wrote in 1751, probably to the Dutch scholar Gronovius:

I had hardly a minute to spend on my once, & indeed future, favourite Studdys having no house no garden near Town; & was almost necessary, to stifle *expellas* &c; I could hold out no longer, so at a very great expense, I repair'd a great house my father had within five miles of Lond; in a situation that yields to none; you may remember hearing of the Villages of Hampstead & Highgate, plac'd on two high hills; the house is betwixt them defended from the north by a great wood; tho in anothers possesion, to the south an old wood of 30 acres belonging to me; over which the whole city with 16 miles of the River appears from every window; a garden of 8 acres betwixt me and the wood, I am filling with evry exotick our climate will protect, & considering I have had but one year to work, the number is very great. Here also I have my Library, Instraments &c. & here I spend a day every week in winter with great satisfaction.

As Bute invites him to reply to 'me at my house in Grosvenor Street London' he presumably only used Kenwood as a second home. Bute's correspondence from December 1752 confirms this seasonal use of Kenwood: 'We came to Town about two weeks from Canewood, and I believe we shall return to it again in two or 3 months at most.'

The correspondence of his mother-in-law, Lady Mary Wortley Montagu, helps to date Bute's move to Kenwood, and confirms Bute's claim that 'at a very great expense, I repair'd a great house'. In 1749 she wrote to Lady Oxford: 'my daughter writes me word she has fitted up that house near Hampstead, which I once had the honour to see with your ladyship; I hope it is a proof that she is in no want of money.' Two days later she wrote to her daughter: 'I very well remember Caenwood House, and cannot wish you a more agreeable place. It would be a great pleasure to me to see my grandchildren run about in the gardens. I do not question Lord Bute's good taste in the improvements round it, or yours in the choice of the furniture.' Fuller details of the architectural repairs, redecoration and furnishing undertaken by Lord and Lady Bute have yet to come to light.

By 1754 the distance from central London

proved too much, and Bute sold the estate to William Murray. The following year Bute wrote from his new residence in South Audley Street 'I have left the country entirely, & am come for my childrens' educ. to settle in Town.' But Bute could not adjust to urban living; he loved gardening and his public position required a 'seat'. In 1762, the year of his appointment as first minister, he purchased Luton Hoo in Bedfordshire, where he employed Robert Adam from 1767.

Bute was first introduced to Adam in May 1758 after Lady Mary Wortley Montagu wrote to Lady Bute from Rome of 'a country-man of yours (Mr Adam) who desires to be introduced to you. He seemed to me, in one short visit, to be a man of genius.' It was through Bute's influence that Adam was appointed (with William Chambers) Architect of the King's Works in 1761. According to Horace Walpole, the Adam brothers became 'attached particularly to Lord Bute and Lord Mansfield'. In 1773 Bute employed Adam again to build Highcliffe on the coast near Christchurch, Dorset, with a conservatory nearly 300 ft long. When Adam published his *Works* in 1774 'Luton House' immediately followed the section on Kenwood. It seems, therefore, most likely that Adam would have worked at Kenwood had Bute remained, and that the architect owed his introduction to Mansfield to Bute.

LORD MANSFIELD,
Chief Justice of England, 1773.

William Murray, 1st Earl of Mansfield *by David Martin, 1775. The portrait commissioned as the Library overmantel is now in the Mansfield family collection at Scone Palace. This replica by the same artist hangs at Kenwood (see page 19).*

# WILLIAM MURRAY, 1st EARL OF MANSFIELD (1705–93)

The circumstances under which Bute sold Kenwood to William Murray, his supporter and fellow Scot, are not yet known, but there were several good reasons why the new Attorney General should acquire the estate. He certainly did not purchase it to pursue a sporting life. The promising lawyer had probably been Bute's guest on occasions. Kenwood was not in the most fashionable Thames-side suburbs of Richmond and Twickenham, but Highgate offered a direct route to the Inns of Court and Westminster, whilst Hampstead provided the pleasures of a fashionable spa town. As his political master, Bute would have advised Murray of the advantages of a suburban villa in which to receive influential guests. A further attraction would have been the classical ideal of a rural retreat, as described by Horace and enjoyed by Mansfield's mentor Alexander Pope. Murray had been a regular guest at the poet's Twickenham villa until Pope's death in 1744. There was also a financial incentive for, by letting out parts of the surrounding estate to neighbouring farmers, Kenwood came to provide him with an additional source of income. He also needed a new home, for there was no prospect of visiting or returning to his family's ancestral seat in Scotland.

From the public's point of view, Kenwood was identified more with Lord Mansfield than with any other resident in the eighteenth century. His reputation as Attorney General from 1754 and as Chief Justice of the Court of King's Bench from 1756 (when he was raised to the peerage) made his house of interest to both his admirers and his enemies. The popular associations Kenwood then carried, as reflected in the numerous engravings of the house published from 1773, and their accompanying texts, can be briefly reconstructed.

## Lord Mansfield's career

Today Lord Mansfield is generally regarded as the greatest British judge of the eighteenth century. Lord Chief Justice for thirty-two years, he is credited with reforming Court procedure, developing commercial law to keep apace with the needs of an expanding empire, and with passing several historic judgements, including the ruling against the rights of slavers over their slaves in England. To his discredit are held his refusal to acknowledge the right to independence of the North American colonies, and his show of indifference at the physical collapse in Parliament of his lifelong foe, William Pitt the Elder, Earl of Chatham.

Best known as a lawyer, Lord Mansfield also held political ambitions. From 1742, when he was appointed Solicitor General at the age of thirty-seven, he worked at the centre of the nation's political affairs. In 1756 his decision not to pursue high office in the House of Commons but to accept the appointment of Lord Chief Justice was bitterly regretted by the first minister of the day, the Duke of Newcastle, who resigned three days later after a desperate effort to retain him. As Attorney General from 1754, Murray had been the ablest defender of the Government against Pitt in the House of Commons. Lord Chesterfield observed:

Mr Pitt and Mr Murray, the Attorney-General are beyond comparison the best speakers. They alone can inflame or quiet the House; they alone are so attended to in that numerous and noisy assembly that you might hear a pin fall while either of them is speaking.

For all his abilities and admirers Murray knew his path to political pre-eminence to be blocked, for he was not only a Scot but a suspected

Jacobite. His father, the 5th Viscount Stormont, and eldest brother, had both been imprisoned after taking part in the Jacobite rising of 1715; and one of his brothers followed the Old Pretender, James Stuart into exile in 1715 and became governor to the Young Pretender, 'Bonnie Prince Charlie'. The latter was received by William Murray's sisters at the family seat, Scone Palace in Perthshire, during the 1745 Rising.

William Murray had left Scone at the age of thirteen, never to return to Scotland. At Westminster School and Oxford University he resolved to support the Hanoverian dynasty, and abandoned the Stuart cause. But fear of the Scots was widespread among Englishmen, not only because of the threat of open rebellion but, more menacingly, because of their success in obtaining positions of power and influence, from Lord Bute down. In 1758 Murray was called before the Lords of the Privy Council to answer charges of Jacobite activities. In 1756 he wrote to Newcastle of his decision to withdraw from the House of Commons, seeing his future there blighted by public opinion of his family: 'If I could bring myself to submit to what I shou'd look upon as my disgrace. . . . I am convinced it wou'd tend to yr dishonour as a man & mine as a minister.'

The shadow of his Scottish Jacobite background hung over all his career. Despite his efforts to adopt an English accent and the oratory lessons of his mentor Alexander Pope, traces of the Scottish origins of 'the silver-tongued Murray' always remained. His architectural improvements to Kenwood can also be seen as part of the continuing efforts of a self-made younger son to establish himself south of the border.

Murray had married into the English aristocracy in 1738, taking as his bride the thirty-four year old daughter of the 2nd Earl of Nottingham and 7th Earl of Winchilsea. When the position of Chief Justice of the Court of King's Bench lay within his grasp, Murray refused to accept it, or even continue as Attorney General, without a peerage, even though the position was a job for life, worth £6,000 a year. Having acquired Kenwood, he used it to meet in private some of the major figures of the day. For example, in 1759 he wrote from Kenwood to a fellow judge:

The Bishop of Durham is now and has been with me since Monday last. Tomorrow I expect the Primate and Lord George Sackville to stay some days so I shall hardly be able to ride to Town any morning before next week. . . . While the company is at cards I play my rubbers at this work, not the pleasantest in the world; but what must be done I have to do.

On 2 September 1759 the Duke of Newcastle wrote to Mansfield: 'I will wait upon you at Kenwood and spend the evening there. But I beg we may have a warm room.' Mansfield's need for

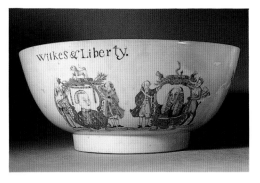

Lord Mansfield's unpopularity is clear from this punch bowl at Kenwood, in which his portrait may be seen beneath a serpent, thistles, and flanked by Lord Bute and the Devil.

a grand reception room and additional bedrooms for house guests must have become apparent, for this is essentially what he commissioned Adam to design five years later.

## Public opinion of Mansfield

Despite his decision not to pursue political office, Mansfield could not avoid being suspected of acting as a 'closet' adviser to the Crown, and his unpopularity grew. John Wilkes' sensationalist newspaper *The North Briton* campaigned against the apparent rule of England by Bute and his fellow Scots to the point of seditious libel. During his trial of Wilkes in 1768, Mansfield received threats in letters and other forms that cannot have strengthened his sense of security. In 1770 both the *Public Advertiser* and *London Evening Post* published an open letter to Mansfield from 'Junius' in which his political and legal activities came under malicious attack. Junius found, for example:

the little prudential policy of a Scotchman. Instead of acting that open and generous part which becomes your rank and station, you merely skulk in the closet, and give your sovereign such advice as you have not spirit to avow or defend. You secretly engross the power, while you decline the title, of minister.

A Scotsman, supposed Jacobite and closet prime minister, Mansfield was also accused of being a Papist. During the 'No-Popery' Gordon Riots of 1780, his carriage windows were smashed outside the Houses of Parliament. According to the *Lords Journal and Parliamentary History* a crowd of 60,000 filled Palace Yard, Westminster and 'Lord Mansfield the Speaker *pro tempore* . . . was very ill treated, and came into the House with his wig dishevelled; Lord Stormont escaped with difficulty, with his life'. Anarchy prevailed over the following days, especially as the rioters released prisoners from jails and so swelled their ranks. Shortly after 9pm on Tuesday 6 June a mob arrived at Mansfield's town house in Bloomsbury Square, brandishing a noose. Lord and Lady Mansfield escaped through a back passage before the rabble made a bonfire of the furniture, tossing Mansfield's collection of classical and medieval manuscripts from the windows. Saving only his dinner bell with which

William Murray, 1st Earl of Mansfield, *enamel miniature by William Russell Birch after the portrait by Reynolds now at Scone Palace. Between 1786 and 1793 Birch painted thirteen miniatures of Lord Mansfield, and became a regular visitor to Kenwood.*

to rally themselves, and armed with his iron railings, they marched to Kenwood, leaving his town house in ashes. Kenwood narrowly escaped the same fate, thanks to the swift action of Mansfield's nephew and heir, Lord Stormont.

In the face of such hatred. Mansfield also achieved popularity and celebrity. The first biography of him appeared only four years after his death, and contained a list of thirteen known portraits. Some were engraved in his own lifetime, and kept by admirers, particularly law students who could observe him at the Court of King's Bench, where crowds would gather to hear him pronounce judgement. Jeremy Bentham, for example, was said to have 'kept, as a great treasure, a picture of him, and frequently went to Caen Wood, as a lover to the shrine of his mistress, in the hope that chance might throw him his way'.

### The 'friend of every elegant art'

Beyond statesmen and lawyers, the range and depth of Mansfield's character was appreciated by the men of letters of his day. To Boswell's prompting comment 'Lord Mansfield is not a mere lawyer' Dr Johnson replied: 'Lord Mansfield when he first came to town, "drank champagne with the wits" as Prior says. He was the friend of Pope.' On the poet's death in 1744 the young lawyer inherited Pope's cherished busts of Homer and of Isaac Newton. Both busts later found a home at Kenwood and are now at Scone. Another poet, Cowper, lamented the destruction of Mansfield's great library in the Gordon Riots:

> And Murray sighs o'er Pope and Swift
> And many a treasure more,
> The well-judged purchase and the gift
> That graced his lettered store.

In his published *Works*, Robert Adam paid tribute to 'Lord Mansfield, the friend of every elegant art and useful science'. However, he had his limitations. Sir Joshua Reynolds' first impression on meeting him in 1769 was marred by Mansfield's 'boyish' endeavours to impress David Garrick. According to Edmund Malone, Reynolds 'was grievously disappointed in finding this *great lawyer* so *little* at the same time'.

There is little evidence to suggest that Mansfield added the role of connoisseur to his accomplishments, and the exceptional free rein Adam enjoyed at Kenwood may reflect a lack of critical interest, as much as any great respect for his genius. This free rein did not benefit from extravagance, however, for Mansfield kept within his means as a patron. Indeed, the wealth of documentation surviving in the Mansfield family papers is evidence of his concern for accurate accounts.

William Murray had not enjoyed the benefits of the customary 'Grand Tour' of Europe as the culmination to his education, due partly to his estrangement from his family at an early age, and partly to his determination to rise as a lawyer without private means. Consequently he had not formed a collection of classical sculptures and old master paintings, nor did he try to acquire one. Nevertheless, as a man of intellect and mounting wealth he became a great bibliophile, and so needed Adam to add a library, rather than a gallery, to house his collection at Kenwood.

Lord Mansfield's collection of paintings seems to have been formed on associative rather than aesthetic principles. It consisted largely of portraits of people he knew or admired, together with amateur copies by his wife's sister Henrietta, Duchess of Cleveland. As a younger son wishing to shed his Jacobite background he is unlikely to have inherited portraits of his ancestors. *The Morning Herald* noted in an article describing Kenwood in 1781: 'the paintings are almost all family pictures, and those in a stile far from the best'. Several of the portraits and drawings listed in the article were in his Dressing Room (see chapter 1). Furniture for Kenwood was supplied initially by William France, and then through Adam by relatively obscure craftsmen working to the architect's designs. No antique sculpture is recorded in Lord Mansfield's house, the Library or 'great room' effectively serving as a gallery where guests might admire the bibliophile's collection.

The same newspaper article describes the two dominant works of art to be admired in this climax to the new reception suite: 'Martin's well known picture of Lord Mansfield, is the only picture in the room. Between the pillars, at the upper end of the room is a bust of his Lordship, with this motto '*Uni Aequus Virtuti*'. Lord Mansfield's motto ('Faithful to Virtue Alone') may still be read on his bust by Nollekens at Kenwood. It is taken from Horace's *Satires*, and was earlier used on Pope's bust by Roubiliac of 1740. This curious temple-like display provided a focus to the vast Library and, indeed, to the virtual cult of Lord Mansfield that emerged.

Lord Mansfield retired as Lord Chief Justice in 1788, four years after the death of his wife, and his last five years were spent at Kenwood, much of it upstairs. His last contribution to Kenwood was to purchase, in 1789, Millfield Farm, to prevent the development of suburban villas. The ninety acres reached just south of Parliament Hill and included Highgate Ponds, bringing the total estate at that time to some 232 acres.

The autobiography of the enamel painter William Russell Birch includes many glimpses of daily life here, ranging from the Earl's morning walks with his resident physician, Dr Combes, to the arrival of Mr French the gardener after dinner proudly bearing a plate piled high with fresh peaches from the Orangery. In earlier times, when Lord Mansfield left regularly for Westminster Hall, Mr French would lay a sweet-smelling nosegay by his breakfast cup of coffee to take with him. According to Birch, George III and Queen Charlotte were frequent visitors.

A final vignette is provided by the novelist Fanny Burney, who visited Kenwood with her eminent father towards the end of Lord Mansfield's life. She noted in her diary:

Poor Lord Mansfield had not been downstairs, the housekeeper told us, for the last four years; yet she asserts he is by no means superannuated, and frequently sees his very intimate friends, and seldom refuses to be consulted by any lawyers. . . . I felt melancholy upon entering his house to recollect how often . . . we had been invited by Miss Murrays, my Lord's nieces. I asked after these ladies and left them my respects. I heard they were upstairs with Lord Mansfield, whom they never left.

Lord Mansfield died on 18 March 1793 and is buried in Westminster Abbey.

## Dido and Lord Mansfield's nieces

Lord and Lady Mansfield had no children of their own, but Kenwood must have echoed with family life, for they adopted two generations of nieces. Anne Murray was the sister of his nephew and heir David, 7th Viscount Stormont. She was probably joined at Kenwood by their sister Marjory. Elizabeth Murray was Lord Stormont's daughter by his first wife and she had as her companion the 'mulatto' Dido Elizabeth Belle, the natural daughter of Mansfield's other nephew Sir John Lindsay, a captain in the Royal Navy. Dido's mother, a black, had been taken prisoner by Sir John in the West Indies and Dido (named after the classical Queen of Carthage) was subsequently born in England.

Dido and Lord Mansfield were on affectionate terms, but she clearly held an ambiguous and uncomfortable status, as neither a servant nor a fully fledged member of the family. For example, on 29 August 1779 an American visitor to Kenwood, Thomas Hutchinson, noted in his diary how after dinner 'a black came in and sat with the ladies, and after coffee walked with the company in the gardens'. He further describes Dido on that summer evening walk as 'a sort of Superintendant over the dairy poultry yard, &c, which we visited'.

Lady Mansfield died in 1784. Elizabeth left the following year to marry her cousin while Anne stayed to keep house for the aged Earl with his steward, John Way. Her account book spanning the last eight years of her uncle's life (1785–93) survives at Kenwood and records daily expenditure on the house and farm in painstaking (and evocative) detail. Entries range from the Highgate Sunday School subscription down to the price of dogs' meat. Servants' wages are also included with the housekeeping expenses. The cook was highly prized, at £50 a year, whereas the rat catcher received only £7 7 shillings and 4 pence.

Payments to Dido are recorded every year in the account book. The eight years spent with her aunts, after the departure of her cousin, cannot have been as carefree, particularly with the ailing health of her guardian and protector. At Lord Mansfield's death in 1793 she was left £500 and an annuity of £100 for life. He also took the precaution of confirming her freedom from slavery in his will. Dido probably left Kenwood shortly after Lord Mansfield's death, when she would have been about thirty; the next year she is referred to in the family account at Hoare's Bank as Mrs Davinier. Her later life still remains a mystery.

*In this double portrait attributed to Zoffany, Lord Mansfield's niece, Elizabeth Murray is shown seated on a garden bench on the terrace at Kenwood. She looks up from her reading while her companion Dido Belle strolls past, carrying fruit from the Orangery and pointing to the colour of her cheek. (The Earl of Mansfield, Scone Palace)*

# DAVID MURRAY, 2nd EARL OF MANSFIELD (1727–96)

When David Murray, 7th Viscount Stormont, succeeded his uncle in 1793 his family's principal title changed and as the 2nd Earl of Mansfield he swiftly set about enlarging Kenwood in preference to the Stormonts' historic Scottish seat, Scone Palace. At 66, he had already enjoyed a distinguished, international career as Ambassador at Vienna (1763–72) and then Paris (1772–78) before returning to Britain in 1778 as Secretary of State for the Northern Department. No doubt he benefited from his uncle's interest.

Despite spending his career abroad, he knew Kenwood well, for his daughter Elizabeth was raised by his uncle after the death of his first wife in 1766 and his sister Anne also lived at Kenwood. In 1780 he saved the house from certain destruction when, as Minister responsible for controlling the Gordon Riots, he ordered 'a detachment of light horse' to intercept the mob that was advancing on the villa. Fortunately the landlord of the Spaniard's Inn was already rendering them insensible with free ale, assisted by Lord Mansfield's steward, who filled tubs by the roadside from his master's cellar. By the time of his uncle's death, the second Earl's plans to transform Kenwood into a substantial family home were well developed, but not matured. Time was short and before he died just three years later he set aside £20,000 in his will for his heir, his young son by his second marriage, to complete the work.

## The second Earl as patron

The second Earl combined his uncle's great learning with the patronage of contemporary painters, cabinet-makers, upholsterers and a sculptor. To commemorate his first marriage in Warsaw in 1759 he commissioned companion portraits of himself and his wife from Bacciarelli. After his wife's early death in 1766 he travelled to Italy and there commissioned his portrait from Batoni. In the opinion of the great antiquarian Winckelmann (whom he met in Rome in 1768) he was 'the most learned man of his rank whom I have yet known'. In 1776 Lord Stormont married the Hon. Louisa Cathcart, thirty-one years his junior, and between 1776 and 1784 he commissioned portraits of himself, his new wife and their son from George Romney.

*The 1st Earl of Mansfield's monument in Westminster Abbey by John Flaxman, completed 1801. (Reproduced by permission of the Dean and Chapter, Westminster Abbey)*

Shortly after their marriage in 1776 Lord and Lady Stormont stayed at Kenwood before he resumed his duties in Paris. Louisa wrote to her sister Mrs Graham (herself the subject of one of Gainsborough's finest portraits):

I am delighted with everything about me. I only regret I can't carry all Lord Stormont's family to Paris. . . . Miss Eliza [her new step-daughter Elizabeth] and I retired after tea. I had a mind to have a little conversation with her and am delighted with her, she is made up of good humour and docility, but Lord Stormont says Lady Mansfield wont hear of letting her go with us, which I regret exceedingly. . . . Lord Stormont and I are now so well acquainted that I wonder how I ever could be afraid of him.

In a later letter she describes her honeymoon host and his nieces:

You did not see enough of Lord Mansfield to know how diverting he is, he says with the gravest face the most comical things imaginable. We are very well together. Lady Mansfield is very agreeable too, and both my sisters extremely so. This place is delightful, I never saw anything I liked more.

After returning to London from Paris in 1778, Lord Stormont followed his uncle's example and commissioned Robert Adam to prepare designs for his town house, 37 Portland Place. His account at Hoare's Bank, opened in 1779, together with his surviving account book at Scone (commenced 1778) reveal numerous payments to the leading cabinet-makers of the day. Artists to whom payments were made for portraits include Romney, Gainsborough and Cosway. He evidently held his uncle in high esteem and shared in the 'cult' that developed around him, purchasing a cast of the first Earl's bust from Nollekens, a cameo from Tassie, and an enamel miniature from Birch as well as subscribing to the engraving of Copley's painting *The Death of Chatham*, in which the first Earl features prominently, conspicuously ignoring the collapse of his life-long foe in Parliament.

On inheriting Kenwood the second Earl employed the landscape painter Julius Caesar Ibbetson virtually as 'artist in residence'. Ibbetson decorated the new Music Room, in which an organ supplied by William Gray held pride of place (see chapter 1). The second Earl also brought his family pictures to Kenwood, clearly intending the villa to be the family's main residence, rather than Scone.

The magnificent French furniture now at Scone Palace was largely acquired by Lord Stormont. The collection may have commenced in 1774 when his uncle stayed at the Embassy and was presented by him to Louis XVI and Marie Antoinette at Versailles; family tradition holds that the Riesener writing table now at Scone was a gift from the Queen to the ambassador. Unfortunately the earliest inventory of Kenwood only dates from 1831, but the description of the Music Room contains several elaborate pieces that reflect the French love of marquetry and gilt mounts, a love shared by the third Earl, who later added to the collection.

The second Earl's outstanding act of patronage was to commission the imposing monument in Westminster Abbey to his uncle, with a legacy from someone who had benefited from one of Mansfield's judgements. In 1793 the second Earl sought advice from Sir William Hamilton as to the best sculptors then in Italy and the latter recommended Canova, noting 'but I think Flaxman has more spirit and will surpass him soon'. The following year Sir William Hamilton wrote of John Flaxman 'I rejoice at your Lordship's having given him so fair a Field to display his genius in England'.

A year before the commission Lord Stormont was a pall bearer at Robert Adam's funeral in Westminster Abbey; he was still corresponding with James Adam in 1793 concerning stucco composition on his house in Portland Place. It is tempting, therefore, to speculate whether the · second Earl might have brought Adam back to Kenwood to enlarge the house in 1793, had the architect not died suddenly. In fact, George Saunders was employed (see chapter 2) and the remodelling of the grounds commenced under the great landscape gardener Humphry Repton (see chapter 5). The end result of this final flourish to a colourful and accomplished life was to leave Kenwood largely as we find it today: one of the capital's finest villas, seemingly set in picturesque seclusion.

# DAVID WILLIAM MURRAY, 3rd EARL OF MANSFIELD (1777–1840)

David William Murray succeeded as the 3rd Earl of Mansfield in 1796, when he was just nineteen years old. The following year he married Frederica, daughter of Dr William Markham, Archbishop of York. Unlike the previous earls, he had little or no political ambition, and he is recorded only as one of twenty-two stalwarts who voted against the third reading of the Reform Bill on 4 June 1832. But as a patron of architects, painters and landscape gardeners he was clearly determined to put his house in order. It was long believed that he neglected Kenwood in favour of the family's Scottish seat. However, documents reveal that he presided over extensive restoration and refurbishment at Kenwood, completing his father's architectural additions with rich 'Regency' interiors.

## Refurbishment at Kenwood

Domestic account books for 1801–02 and 1807–08 preserved at Kenwood record payments to the fashionable upholsterers and cabinet-makers of the day. In 1801 bills were submitted by Gillow and by Paxter of Hampstead. From 1807–08 payments were made to J. Weston, Tatham & Bayley and to Nicholas Morel, all of whom at various times supplied furnishings to the Prince of Wales, later George IV, either at Windsor Castle or at Carlton House. Substantial restoration and redecoration was undertaken at Kenwood from 1815 to 1817, and is recorded in craftsmen's accounts preserved at Scone. In addition to general cleaning and repairs the entrance hall was remodelled following the discovery of rotten timbers and all the Orangery windows were replaced. Throughout the house, doors, dados and shutters were grained to resemble oak, and both sets of staircase ballusters were bronzed. Adam's mirrored recesses in the Library were filled with bookshelves and the columns and pilasters in the Ante Chamber were painted in imitation of porphyry. Several rooms were newly papered or painted 'with Corner Ornaments &c'.

The architect responsible for the restoration and redecoration was William Atkinson. A pupil of Wyatt and architect to the Ordnance Office, he first worked for the third Earl at Scone Palace, which he effectively rebuilt. In June 1817 he learnt that Lord Mansfield's steward at Kenwood, Mr Hunter, had complained to his patron of delays, and this prompted the architect to write a lengthy and heated justification of all his work there. His letter reveals the surprisingly shoddy construction that Adam and Saunders permitted, or passed over:

the greater part of the expense you have now been put to, has been owing to the Dry Rot and that occasioned in a great measure, either by the ignorance or inattention of the former Architects to the House – or by their Employers not giving time for the walls to dry before they were inclosed by plastering . . . and owing to timber having been built into the walls in so many parts of the house where it had perished, this occasioned new solid brickwork to secure the walls. . . . There were many parts of the house difficult to manage to make secure such as Bed Rooms over kitchen, taking away partition in new Book Room – constructing two new stoves to warm staircases and Anti Rooms and building up new wall of House under the Portico so as to prevent it settling from the old walls besides securing the walls in many parts where they were very weak and insecure – I am certain there never was any work done that has stood better and I certainly expected to have got some credit from your Lordship.

The earliest inventory, drawn up in 1831, provides a vivid impression of the furnished rooms in the third Earl's day. For example, the Dining Room was hung with '4 Elegant scarlet cloth window curtains & draperies boardered with black velvet and yellow gold coloured lace'

*David Murray, 7th Viscount Stormont, later 2nd Earl of Mansfield. This line engraving is an illustration from the* London Magazine, *1780.*

(see chapter 1). The third Earl's account at Hoare's Bank further reveals him as a patron, honouring his father's commissions to Saunders and Flaxman. There are also payments to Joseph Bonomi (for structural repairs to the Library) in 1799, to George Stubbs in 1802 and to Hoppner and Wilkie the following year.

Hoppner painted the third Earl and his wife, and Wilkie found his first patron and fame (but not fortune) with his celebrated painting in the spirit of Teniers, *The Village Politicians* (still in the Mansfield collection at Scone). Prompted by his mother, the third Earl 'discovered' Wilkie, for he asked the artist to paint this picture of an alehouse debate, after seeing a sketch on his easel. Artist and patron soon quarrelled over the price, however, and only after it made Wilkie's successful debut at the Royal Academy in 1806 did the Earl reluctantly agree to pay him 30 guineas, double the price first mentioned. This experience did not turn him totally against the patronage of modern art. In 1820 and 1823 John Linnell came to Kenwood, commissioned by the third Earl to copy miniatures of his daughters.

When J. Norris Brewer described the house in detail in *London and Middlesex* (1816) he pointed out 'In several apartments contiguous to the library are some pictures, among which we noticed two large and fine landscapes, supposed by Claude; a piece by Teniers; and Wilkie's *Village Politicians*. In the *Billiard Room* are several good family portraits.' The latter, now known as the Upper Hall, was redecorated at this time. Not all the best pictures were at Kenwood, however, for the third Earl had acquired Titian's *Baldassare Castiglione* (National Gallery, Ireland) in 1800 and chose to hang it at Scone.

Brewer's account also includes a lengthy description of the pleasure grounds, which further confirms the activity at Kenwood in these years. Adjacent lay Lord Mansfield's 'farm of about two hundred acres, which is in a very high state of cultivation', all 'under the guidance of Mr. Hunter, who resides on the estate as landsteward to the Earl of Mansfield, and who was likewise retained as steward by the Lord Chief Justice'.

Correspondence between Edward Hunter and the third Earl during the latter's absence in France and Rome in 1818 reveals the scale of daily activity on the estate, as well as the quantity of foreign flowers, vegetables, vines, wheat and fruit trees sent by Lord Mansfield to his overwhelmed steward (see chapter 5). He also sent home from France porcelain, wine and fine furniture. Meanwhile Hunter writes for instructions on staff shortages and whether the new dog and bitch and their nine puppies should be sent to Scone or drowned.

**A royal visit**
The years of repair, redecoration and cultivation

under the third Earl must have made Kenwood fit for a king, or at least for some wealthy suitors for the third Earl's four daughters. A Russian Grand Duke visited Kenwood in 1818 (see below) and on 23 July 1835 William IV and Queen Adelaide paid a royal visit. The press reported:

There were at one time upwards of 800 of the nobility and gentry in the park, in the marquees and on the lawn, where the band of the 1st Regiment of Life Guards was in attendance. . . . At an early hour in the evening their Majesties partook of a sumptuous *déjeuné* in the banqueting-room . . . a brilliant display of fireworks and illuminations concluded the festivities of the day.

This colourful association, complete with a 'strawberry feast', was reported rather differently by Fanny Gascoyne-Cecil, Marchioness of Salisbury in her diary:

The grounds are excessively pretty, and if there had been enough to eat, it would have been perfect. . . . The King and Queen and all the Royalties seemed extremely well pleased: the King in particular trotted about with Lord M. in the most active manner, and made innumerable speeches!

Two years later she made a similar complaint: 'Breakfast at Ken Wood. No men, and few eatables; very dull.'

# THE LATER EARLS AT KENWOOD

William David Murray, 4th Earl of Mansfield (1806–98) succeeded his father in 1840. He had a successful career in the House of Commons, and was even considered by some to be a future prime minister until the early death of his wife in 1837 led to his temporary withdrawal from public life. He later became known as the 'Father to the House of Lords'. He preferred Scone, but spent three months of each year at Kenwood. In 1889 he sold 201 acres of the Kenwood estate, comprising Parliament Hill Fields and part of the Elms Estate, to the Metropolitan Board of Works to enlarge Hampstead Heath, and on his death fears grew of the sale of the remainder to developers.

In these years Kenwood became a haven for wildlife driven off the heath by pleasure trippers, as the arrival of the railway at South End Green in 1860 turned ''Appy Ampstead' into a cockney pleasure ground, with an estimated 100,000 people arriving by train from the East End on a fine day in the 1880s. The house was not entirely dormant, however. In 1843 the fourth Earl held a grand *fête champêtre*, with Prince Albert and the Duke of Wellington among the guests of honour, and servants were always busy maintaining the estate. According to William Howitt's *Northern Heights* (1869):

A custom is kept up here which smacks of the old feudal times. Every morning, when the night-watchman goes off duty, at six o'clock, he fires a gun, and immediately three long winds are given on a horn to call the servants, gardeners and labourers to their employment. The horn is blown again at breakfast and dinner hours, and at six in the evening for their dismissal.

Kenwood enjoyed a new lease of life under the fifth Earl, 'the most eligible bachelor in London' who entertained on a grand scale. But only eight years after inheriting the family titles and estates from his grandfather, William David Murray (1860–1906) died suddenly of pneumonia, unmarried. Had he lived, Kenwood's fate might have been very different, for his brother, Alan David Murray (1864–1935), the sixth Earl, followed their father in preferring to live at Scone. He did, however, introduce electric lighting to Kenwood in 1907; hitherto only wax-candles had been used as the successive Earls disdained to use gas-lighting.

At first Kenwood was let to tenants, but subsequently the estate was saved from speculative developers after a lengthy campaign by individuals, associations and the London boroughs.

# GRAND DUKE MICHAEL MICHAELOVITCH (1861–1929)

High on the ridge of Kenwood's North Wood, between the house and Hampstead Lane, two small stone memorial tablets can be found among the undergrowth to one side of the secluded footpath. The inscription on one reads 'Sleep on old friend' and marks the grave of Bill, who died on 20 September 1915, while alongside we are asked to remember Mac, 'An old and faithful friend'. These dogs' graves are the only visible mementoes of the residence at Kenwood of His Imperial Highness Grand Duke Michael Michaelovitch of Russia.

Grand Duke Michael was the great-great-grandson of Catherine the Great, grandson of Tsar Nicholas I and second cousin of Nicholas II, the last of the Tsars. Born at Peterhof, he rose to become Lieut-Colonel of the Caucasian Sharpshooters and a Chevalier of the Black Eagle. Tall, with clear-cut features and a small Greek beard, he was a suggested suitor for Princess Mary of Teck, but nothing came of the suggestion and she is now better known as

Queen Mary, wife of King George V. In 1891 Grand Duke Michael was exiled from Russia for his morganatic marriage to Sophie, Countess of Merenberg (created Countess Torby) a great-granddaughter of Pushkin. They travelled in France and England, enjoying high society life, settling at Keele Hall, Staffordshire and wintering at the Villa Kasebeck in Cannes. According to *The Lady's Realm* (1907–08) the decree of exile was rescinded, but the couple chose to remain in England 'because the position of the charming lady whom he has made his wife would be less pleasant in Russia than it is over here or on the Riviera, where he and Countess Torby are the uncrowned king and queen of Cannes society'. They moved to Kenwood in 1910, to entertain on the grandest scale and raise their three children, Zia, Nada and Michael.

Quite how the Grand Duke came to choose Kenwood as his next home is still unknown, but he was not the first member of the Russian royal family to admire the villa. In the stores of the State Hermitage Museum, Leningrad, a slop bowl decorated with a view of Kenwood records the visit in 1818 of the Grand Duke Michael Pavlovich (grandson of Catherine the Great and brother of Alexander I and Nicholas I). Aged twenty, this Grand Duke had been accompanied by Sir William Congreve (a close associate of the Prince Regent) on his Grand Tour, and as a souvenir he commissioned the Chamberlain-Worcester breakfast and tea service, of which the slop bowl forms a part. On 9 August 1818 the 3rd Earl of Mansfield's steward wrote from his Scottish estate: 'The Grand Duke Michael of

Russia went through Scone House this day with five other Gentlemen on their way to Blair.'

Negotiations with the sixth Earl had begun in June 1908, but it was not until 1 March 1910 that the Grand Duke Michael moved into Kenwood, after a 21-year lease on the furnished property had been signed, at an annual rent of £2,200. Once again, Kenwood became the setting for family life and glamorous society parties. In 1913 an eight-page article in *Country Life* devoted to 'Kenwood, Hampstead The residence of H.I.H. The Grand Duke Michael of Russia' marked the villa's return to public prominence. The nine illustrations of the well furnished rooms (as they appeared before the auction of 1922) have since become a priceless historical record. The luxurious interior of Kenwood at this time is further recorded in a set of photographs of the Upper Hall, the Breakfast Room and the Music Room, the latter including an oil painting of the Grand Duke by Galeoto (illustrated in chapter 1). On 11 March 1911 *The Graphic* reported 'The Grand Duke has been a stranger to his own country since his marriage, but here he is a personal favourite with the Royal family, and his elder daughter Countess Anastasia (Zia) Torby, born in 1892, is to be one of the debutantes of the present season'. On a sadder note, the writer observed that, but for his marriage, the Grand Duke 'might not now be occupying Kenwood, but be gazing on the Neva instead of the pond on Hampstead Heath'.

Confirmation of the glittering cosmopolitan world they brought to Kenwood is provided by an account in the *Hampstead and Highgate Express* (13 June 1914) of a royal dinner and ball, attended by most of aristocratic Society from the King and Queen down. For example: 'The

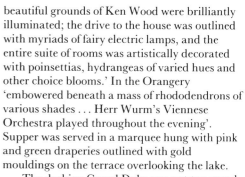

beautiful grounds of Ken Wood were brilliantly illuminated; the drive to the house was outlined with myriads of fairy electric lamps, and the entire suite of rooms was artistically decorated with poinsettias, hydrangeas of varied hues and other choice blooms.' In the Orangery 'embowered beneath a mass of rhododendrons of various shades . . . Herr Wurm's Viennese Orchestra played throughout the evening'. Supper was served in a marquee hung with pink and green draperies outlined with gold mouldings on the terrace overlooking the lake.

The dashing Grand Duke was not too grand for local village life and he participated in several good causes. In 1912 he became President of the Hampstead General Hospital and the following year he presented it with a motor ambulance, the first of its kind in London outside the City. In July 1914 he opened a new high-diving board at Highgate Ponds, with the intention of training athletes for the next Olympic Games, war permitting. At the outbreak of war the Grand Duke and his daughters ran a campaign to collect 500,000 pairs of socks and mittens for the troops at the Front; he also attended a 'cinema entertainment' at Highgate Electric Palace with his wife and the actress Ellen Terry to raise funds for the Highgate War Charities.

The Grand Duke and Lord Mansfield offered Kenwood for use as a war hospital, and in November 1915 the Royal Naval Anti-Aircraft Mobile Brigade was established in the stable block, under Commander A. Rawlinson RNVR. Officers and men quartered in the stable barracks slept in hammocks and played cricket in the grounds of Kenwood, before going on night-patrol with their searchlights and high-angle anti-aircraft cannons mounted on Lancia lorries, ready to take on the Zeppelins. They also had the use of the golf course, newly created in 1909 for the Grand Duke (the reigning President of the Cannes Golf Club) in the meadow beyond the South Wood.

Commander Rawlinson later published his memoirs, in which he recalled with no sense of irony the pleasures of joining the Grand Duke and his daughters for breakfast after the more interesting air-raids:

It became my custom, after any specially interesting raid, to go across to the Grand Duke's house at Kenwood, where I always received a cordial welcome, to have breakfast, and during that meal to tell them the various incidents of the night.

On those occasions the contrast between the atmosphere of that happy family home, and that of the miserable districts in which so much of our work was done, was most striking. For, even if the conditions in the East End of London during the raids were exceptionally miserable, there is no doubt that conditions at the Grand Ducal breakfast-table were exceptionally enjoyable; and the most remarkable beauty and charm of the ladies, as well as the deep interest which all invariably displayed in the events of

*The Royal Naval Anti-Aircraft Mobile Brigade was stationed at Kenwood in 1915–16, during the residence of Grand Duke Michael.*

the night, served to emphasize the contrast in a manner of which I shall always retain a most vivid and delightful recollection.

In August 1916 the brigade moved to Norfolk and in November the same year Kenwood saw the wedding reception of the Grand Duke's younger daughter Countess Nada and Prince George of Battenburg (elder brother of the late Earl Mountbatten of Burma and uncle of Prince Philip). King George, Queen Mary and other members of the royal family were among the guests. The following year on 20 July 1917, Countess Zia married Harold Wernher (later Sir Harold Wernher, Bt. of Luton Hoo) in the Chapel Royal, St James's Palace, with 'half the peerage in addition to royalty present', according to *The Tatler*. The remarkable Fabergé collection for which the Wernher Collection at Luton Hoo is famous today was originally formed by Grand Duke Michael, who purchased pieces direct from the Russian jeweller in St Petersburg. A shadow must have been cast over the marriage by the Russian Revolution, in which the Grand Duke lost his brother, Grand Duke George, and his fortune.

Shortly before the second wedding, with their two daughters' future in English society secured, the Grand Duke and Countess Torby left Kenwood for Cambridge Gate, Regent's Park and the last days of family life at Kenwood came to a close. He died in 1929 at 41 York Terrace, Regent's Park and is buried in Hampstead Cemetery, Fortune Green Road, together with his wife and their son. Count Michael Torby died unmarried in 1959 after a career as an artist, specialising in fashion and theatrical design.

## AN AMERICAN MILLIONAIRESS

The Russian connection continued under Kenwood's next tenant, Nancy Leeds (née Stewart). The widow of an American tin-plate manufacturer, she was left £8 million on the death of her first husband, William B. Leeds. Their son, William B. Leeds Jnr. ('the Tin Plate Croesus') married in 1922 Princess Xenia, younger daughter of Grand Duke George Michaelovitch, brother of Grand Duke Michael. The couple were divorced in 1930 after falling out over Princess Xenia's support of Mrs Anna Anderson's claim to be Tsar Nicholas' daughter Anastasia. After leaving Kenwood Mrs Leeds married Prince Christopher of Greece in 1920. She clearly had a taste for London society, for she also rented Spencer House, Green Park (the Spencer Suite is on loan to Kenwood).

*Poster designed by Percy Fearon ('Poy') in 1921 for the Kenwood Preservation Council's appeal to save the house and estate from suburban development.*

## THE SAVING OF KENWOOD

Following the end of the First World War the 6th Earl of Mansfield received several offers for the estate and in 1919 the Kenwood Preservation Committee was formed. On 20 October 1920 an agreement was drawn up between Lord Mansfield and the Committee (represented by Sir Arthur Crosfield, Sir Herbert Nield and Sir Robert Waley Cohen) for the sale of the house and estate for £340,000, payable before 1 December 1921. This bid to save Kenwood failed, and the contents of the house were sold at auction from 6 November 1922. The next month the Committee succeeded in completing the purchase of 100 acres, including the meadowlands and Grand Duke Michael's golf course between Parliament Hill Fields and the South Wood. The South Wood, together with the lakes (a total of 32 acres) was purchased and vested in the London County Council in 1924, and on 18 July 1925 'Ken Wood' was opened to the public by King George V. The same year the house and remaining 74 acres were acquired by Edward Cecil Guinness, 1st Earl of Iveagh, at the reduced price of £107,900. Lord Iveagh intended to bequeath Kenwood to the nation on his death or after a decade, but in the event, death came first, just two years later. In 1928 a new chapter in the history of Kenwood began to unfold, when the villa opened to the public as the home of Lord Iveagh's magnificent collection.

*'Guinness Trust' by Leslie Ward ('Spy'), published in* Vanity Fair, *1891. The second richest man in England, Edward Cecil Guinness, 1st Earl of Iveagh, saved Kenwood in 1925, just two years before his death.*

*Chapter Four*

# THE COLLECTIONS

When The Iveagh Bequest, Kenwood opened its doors to the public for the first time on Wednesday 18 July 1928 the house and its contents were intended to present 'a fine example of the artistic home of a gentleman of the eighteenth century'. This is how the Act of Parliament establishing the independent museum in 1929 described its character, according to the wishes of Edward Cecil Guinness, 1st Earl of Iveagh (1847–1927) and his trustees. However, the original contents had been dispersed at auction in 1922, after the finest pieces had been removed by the Mansfield family. The entire collection on display in 1928 had been in the house less than three years, and most of Lord Iveagh's paintings had been purchased between 1887 and 1891 without Kenwood in mind. By modern museum standards the stated intention seems most misleading. Visiting Kenwood today, whether drawn by the architecture of Robert and James Adam, the contribution to legal history of the 1st Earl of Mansfield, or by the great paintings acquired by the 1st Earl of Iveagh, we should bear in mind that the magnificent contents are not original to Kenwood, nor, indeed, are they even an eighteenth-century collection.

Kenwood's collections appeal on many levels today. The paintings provide a partial view of Dutch and Flemish art of the seventeenth century, and of British art of the late eighteenth century. They reveal that the taste of Lord Iveagh was typical of a generation of transatlantic collectors active from around 1890 to 1925, buying in the boom years of British art sales. The furniture illustrates the wider activity and influence of Kenwood's architect, Robert Adam, whilst evoking some idea of each room's original appearance and use; the collection features some of the original Kenwood furniture, following its recent rediscovery in North America. The prints, drawings, jewellery, shoe buckles, miniatures and books have a more specialist appeal.

As the collections continue to grow, enhancing the relationship between the architecture and the museum objects within, they are aided by a new generation of soft furnishings historically reconstructed to the highest standard. Kenwood now benefits from over half a century of progress in museum methods, historical research and collecting, and yet the spirit of the Act is still preserved.

The Flower Gatherers *by François Boucher, the first painting purchased by Lord Iveagh (detail).*

In 1886 Guinness Breweries, the largest brewery in the world, became a public company and Edward Cecil Guinness, a multi-millionaire at forty-three, retired as sole proprietor but remained as Chairman. The following year he began to collect paintings in earnest, through just one Bond Street gallery. According to *The Times* (30 August 1938):

Lord Iveagh's associations with Agnews were quite accidental. One day at luncheon time when the partners were at luncheon, Lord Iveagh strolled into a Bond Street gallery and asked to be shown some fine pictures. The cautious assistant refused to show him any, and, considerably piqued, Lord Iveagh left the gallery. Reaching Agnews he entered and made the same request. There, too, he found the partners absent, but the assistant showed greater discernment and there and then sold Lord Iveagh several pictures. Thenceforward Agnews enjoyed practically his exclusive patronage.

The two pictures purchased in that auspicious lunch hour (on 23 June 1887) now hang at Kenwood: *The Flower Gatherers* by Boucher and *View of Dordrecht* by Cuyp. The relationship with Agnews flourished until, four years later, he had acquired some 240 paintings and drawings through their offices to furnish his vast town house in Grosvenor Place, Mayfair.

Like the 1st Earl of Mansfield, Lord Iveagh earned his own title after overcoming the difficulties of rising through the British class system without being born in England. Indeed, both men were handicapped by their nationality: Mansfield by the Jacobite rebellions in Scotland and Iveagh by the Home Rule movement in Ireland. For Iveagh, his collection of paintings was an essential ingredient in that rise, partly as suitable furnishing for his magnificent parties attended by the nobility. Unlike Mansfield, Iveagh had no aspirations to hold public office. After several major social and political benefactions and the expansion of his hospitality through the acquisition of the Elveden estate in Suffolk, he was raised to the peerage in 1891 and was ennobled as Earl of Iveagh and Viscount Elveden in 1919. At his death in 1927 Iveagh was reported to be the second richest man in the country, even after his years of philanthropy and the creation of several family trusts. The duties levied on his remaining estate, valued at £11,000,000, enabled Winston Churchill, as Chancellor of the Exchequer, to lower the standard level of income tax.

## Lord Iveagh's paintings

On Monday 6 November 1922, C. B. King Ltd of Hampstead commenced the auction of the 'Choice & Valuable Furnishing ... within Kenwood Mansion'. The sale spanned four days and included 1,092 lots, ranging from most of the original furniture designed for Kenwood by Robert Adam down to the lino. Many of the more important items had been removed by the owner, Alan David Murray, 6th Earl of Mansfield, to his Perthshire seat, Scone Palace. Here they may still be seen, saved from the obscurity that has enshrouded almost every item dispersed by the sale. When Lord Iveagh purchased the house and 74 acres in 1925 all that remained of the Adam furnishings were the two vast pier glasses still in the library and the adjacent curtain cornices. But this empty shell was precisely what Lord Iveagh needed to house his own collection.

## The society portraits

Despite the apparent haste and amount of outside advice taken to form his collection, Edward Cecil Guinness clearly followed his own taste and principles. The sixty-three paintings listed in the Kenwood Act may be divided into three distinct groups. British portraits of the second half of the eighteenth century make up

the lion's share, and it is for these great society beauties, be they singers, courtesans, royal mistresses, actresses or aristocrats, that Kenwood is best known today. Among the sixteen works by Reynolds, seven by Gainsborough and six by Romney, to be seen at Kenwood, few men will be found. Unlike many aspiring aristocrat collectors Lord Iveagh was clearly not motivated by 'ancestor gathering'. Dazzling ladies are rivalled only by enchanting children, particularly Raeburn's *Sir George Sinclair as a Boy* and Lawrence's *Miss Murray*.

In Reynolds' portraits beauty takes many forms, ranging from the epitome of childhood innocence in the *Brummell Children* frolicking with a mischievous puppy, to the seductive glance of *'Kitty' Fisher as Cleopatra*. Paintings commissioned by gentlemen admirers also include Romney's two portraits of *Emma Hart* in rather less appropriate roles: as a peasant lady industrious at her spinning wheel, and at prayer.

For many visitors, the most striking image in the Kenwood collection is Gainsborough's *Mary, Countess Howe*. Unlike her more theatrical neighbours, she merely strolls through a landscape park, her pink silk costume rustling, her lace apron gently folded back by the breeze, her natural beauty simply enhanced by a pearl choker and earrings, black silk bracelet and straw bonnet. Gazing at one of Gainsborough's most admired works, we are reminded by the artist's elegant brushwork that this ideal of eighteenth-century feminine beauty is, somehow, simply paint on canvas.

## The 'old masters'

Major paintings of international standing will be found among the second distinct group in the collection; indeed, many visitors are surprised to find images familiar from countless reproductions quietly hanging at Kenwood, rather than in the National Gallery. The 'old master' paintings are predominantly drawn from the seventeenth-century Dutch and Flemish schools, with portraits and figure subjects by Rembrandt, Bol, Hals, Snyders, Van Dyck and Vermeer, and landscapes and marine paintings by Ostade, Cuyp, the Van de Veldes and Wynants. This aspect of the Bequest was clearly intended to be analagous to the collecting taste of an eighteenth-century English gentleman, and so complement the portraits of beauties and children. Once again, Lord Iveagh's personal interests prevailed over any academic conventions. This Protestant businessman's taste clearly excluded from the Bequest any grand mythological, historical or religious subject pictures that might seem more at home in Roman Catholic cathedrals or the palaces of Italian princes, than in the house of a successful merchant.

The two supreme masterpieces that crown this aspect of Lord Iveagh's bequest are Rembrandt's *Self Portrait*, painted around 1663 (see page 25); and *The Guitar Player* by Vermeer, from about 1672 (see page 26). Both arrest and enthrall our wandering gaze, but each in a different way. Rembrandt seems to stir and sweep the paint to discover, within his own age-worn features and artist's clothes, some common ground between body and spirit. His gaze seems at once both introspective and triumphant, as he confronts us across the centuries. X rays have revealed that the sketchy group of palette, brushes and maulstick were originally painted in his opposite hand, as in the reversed mirror image he worked from; his other hand reached across to paint on a tilted canvas, just shown as a wedge on the right of the actual painting. Together with some enhancement of his features in the finished work, these changes produced a portrait of the artist for posterity, steady as a rock, instead of a study in a studio mirror. To complete the image, two great arcs painted on the wall behind are thought to allude to the artist's genius, through the legends of the great painters Apelles and Giotto, both of whom could draw a perfect circle freehand. Other explanations put forward for the arcs include the more prosaic idea that they are the unfinished double-hemispheres of a wall map commonly found in Dutch homes at this time. Whatever their meaning (if any) they are essential to the strength of the composition.

Like Rembrandt, Vermeer is a painter's painter, fascinated with the pictorial values of light, colour, volume and form, and the means of relating them to create harmonious compositions. His world, however, is one of perfect, poetic, still-lives, not of psychological dramas. He paints light falling on a precisely posed model and guitar with the disciplined eye we would expect of a scientist, and with a patient dexterity more associated with someone accustomed to painting porcelain. Rembrandt explores the physical potential of his paint using everything from a thick palette-knife to lay in the white turban, to the wooden tip of his brush handle to scribble in the wet paint of his shirt front. Vermeer, by contrast, defines a carefully calculated group with crisp brushwork, creating an effect of simplicity that masks the subtleties involved in balancing an off-centre composition; the sitter, her face in shadow, gazes off to one side with her elbow cropped where the canvas ends.

The typical black 'Dutch ripple' frame heightens the qualities of Vermeer's cool grey light. Kenwood's Rembrandt probably acquired its present 'old master' frame whilst in a French collection in the eighteenth century. Both artists were admired by Reynolds on his tour of the Low Countries in 1781, but whereas Rembrandt was a household name among collectors by the time Iveagh bought the portrait in 1888, Vermeer had only recently been discovered when Iveagh purchased *The Guitar Player* in 1889. In these two paintings at Kenwood you may explore in peace probably the most famous of all Rembrandt's self-portraits, hanging opposite the only Vermeer in this country outside the National Gallery and the Royal Collection.

The third, and smallest, group of paintings represents French art of the Rococo period. Two idyllic *Fêtes Champêtres* by Pater show elegant society at leisure, while in three decorative fantasies by Boucher rustics gather flowers and fruit, and consider harvesting one another.

## Notable omissions

Besides recalling that this magnificent collection is highly personal, of its time, and not original to the Kenwood known to Mansfield and Adam, visitors should bear in mind that the British paintings do not present an historical survey, such as one might find at the Tate Gallery or the Yale Center for British Art. Notable omissions are conversation pieces by Hogarth, Zoffany or Devis (although Lord Iveagh did own Hogarth's satirical *Taste in High Life*); historical and mythological subject paintings by Fuseli (this genre is now represented by works by Angelica Kauffman from the E. E. Cook collection); horse-racing subjects (Stubbs is conspicuously absent); and landscapes by Richard Wilson or Wright of Derby (Claude de Jongh's *Old London Bridge* of 1630 is an exception). Some of these gaps were originally filled by the prints and drawings included in the Bequest, such as Malton's views of Dublin. Loans from the Guinness family also enhanced the collection in its early years. The nineteenth century, for example, was more fully represented by Landseer's *The Stag at Bay* (returned 1951), *The Orphans* by Millais (returned 1968) and *Thetis* by G. F. Watts (returned 1951). Whilst the marine paintings in the collection include a great Turner, long known as *The Iveagh Seapiece*, Lord Iveagh never acquired a work by Constable. Iveagh also lived at Heath House, Hampstead, so we might expect him to have sought out one of Constable's views of Hampstead Heath, but such subjects were, evidently, unsuited to the image of himself and English country life that he wished to present. These and other omissions were no loss to the vision of Georgian elegance he sought to create, and ultimately bequeathed to us with his collection of paintings and Kenwood.

Fishermen upon a Lee Shore in Squally Weather *by J. M. W. Turner, 1802. Also known as* The Iveagh Seapiece.

## Comparable collections

The product of its time, Lord Iveagh's bequest may be better understood through close comparison with the contemporary American collections of Henry E. Huntington (1850–1927), John McFadden (1851–1921) and Henry Clay Frick (1849–1919), to be seen today in public galleries in San Marino, Philadelphia and New York, respectively. The similarity was noted in Iveagh's own lifetime, and on 1 November 1927 *The Times* observed: 'For many years Lord Iveagh has been forming his collection not only in competition with the greatest of the American millionaires but very much on the same lines.'

Like his rival collectors, Edward Cecil Guinness benefited from the economic struggle of the landed gentry at the end of the nineteenth century. The agricultural depression led to the Settled Land Act of 1883, by which family collections previously prevented from sale by laws of entail could be broken up. The discreet endeavours of dealers, particularly Agnew, and later Duveen, brought heirlooms to a new generation of competing collectors with a taste for English portraiture.

These collectors shared a romantic, escapist, vision of Georgian high society, and wished to be associated with its elegance, particularly by posterity, for whom they founded their museums and country house galleries. The generation of millionaires-turned-philanthropists to which Lord Iveagh belonged competed as art collectors in the heyday of British eighteenth-century art, setting many record prices that still seem outstanding today. Fortunately, Lord Iveagh purchased his great full-length portraits a decade or more before his transatlantic rivals followed the fashion. But for the committed collecting of

Lord Iveagh, most of the paintings to be seen at Kenwood today would undoubtedly be in museums and private collections in North America.

## Lord Iveagh's furniture collection

Similar opportunities existed for collectors of Georgian furniture at this time with great house sales (Kenwood included). The market for Georgian furniture was established by the 1880s and with the demand for fine pieces English furniture history developed. Hitherto most collectors had preferred French furniture, resulting in the opulent interiors created at Kenwood in the early nineteenth century, and later at Hertford House (the Wallace Collection) and Waddesdon. As the century drew to a close a new appreciation of English satinwood and marquetry furniture emerged. Adam held a particular appeal. The 'Adams Revival', accelerated by the furniture makers Wright and Mansfield from 1867, led to the publication of selections of plates from the Adam brothers' *Works* in 1880 and 1883 and in 1902–03 all three volumes were reprinted. Most leading manufacturers began to supply 'Adams' furniture (either reproductions or more Victorian compilations) as demand exceeded supply. Several major publications and articles appeared in the opening decades of the present century, particularly in *Country Life* and the *Dictionary of English Furniture* (1924–27).

Collectors of English furniture emerged on both sides of the Atlantic. For example, the soap magnate Sir William Lever, later Lord Leverhulme, lived at Hill House by Hampstead Heath from 1904 until his expanding collection forced him to found his museum at Port Sunlight. It opened in 1922, complete with an 'Adam' room. Had he not founded this museum, it is tempting to speculate whether Lever might have acquired Kenwood.

Despite such opportunities the furniture Iveagh bequeathed with Kenwood included many Edwardian reproductions or over-restored Irish Georgian pieces supplied by P. J. Walsh of Dublin. Most of it is now in store and may be viewed by specialists by appointment. We should not dismiss it as evidence that Iveagh was poorly advised, lacking the equivalent of Agnews in paintings. The finest furniture remained in his family seat at Elveden, Suffolk, at Iveagh House, Dublin and his London town house in Grosvenor Place. Elveden included furnished period rooms, ranging from Early Georgian and French to the 'Adams' style. The most notable piece was a vast and magnificent medal cabinet designed by Sir William Chambers (and carved by Sefferin Alken) for the 1st Earl of Charlemont in 1767, and now in the Courtauld Institute of Art. Lord Iveagh had acquired it in Dublin for use in his dressing room at Elveden. Other fine pieces

Miss Murray *by Sir Thomas Lawrence, 1825–7. Lawrence was keen to paint the Duke of Wellington's god-daughter before her 'rare' beauty changed. He later remarked 'I know of no work by which my reputation would be better supported.'*

occasionally resurface on the art market with an Iveagh provenance. In Dublin, Iveagh House on St Stephens Green still contains the 'Adam room' fully decorated some forty years before the acquisition of Kenwood.

In a codicil to his will, quoted in the Iveagh Bequest (Kenwood) Act, Lord Iveagh expressed 'my hope that Kenwood House may be used permanently for the exhibition of pictures tapestries furniture and the like'. The importance attached to tapestries reflects the influence of leading French and English dealers in this field whom he consulted. Iveagh was also something of a connoisseur of carpets, even if he did buy in the high street (through Harvey Nichols and Liberty's) rather than in Bond Street.

Initially Lord Iveagh sought advice from Joseph Duveen, who resented his acquisition of paintings through Agnew. But his main adviser became Caspar Purdon Clarke, who accompanied Lord and Lady Iveagh on buying visits to France in search of tapestries. This Keeper of the Indian Section at the South Kensington Museum later became director of the renamed Victoria and Albert Museum and subsequently of the Metropolitan Museum of Art in New York.

In his introduction to *Pictures from the Iveagh Bequest* (1928) Sir Charles Holmes (the Director of the National Gallery) quoted a personal recollection of Lord Iveagh written by one of his close associates. Once again emphasis is clearly given to Iveagh's personal love of the decorative arts, a love still overshadowed today by the collection of paintings he assembled through Agnews:

from early days he began to purchase things of beauty, here a piece of tapestry, there a piece of sculpture or old furniture, an occasional picture or engraving, a jewel, a piece of old embroidery, a fine carpet. He built extensively, and under sound advice as far as the outside of his houses were concerned, but he dealt with the interiors from his own knowledge and taste. . . . His interests took him to London in the early eighties, and there the acquisition of a town house necessitated the purchase of more furniture, and above all pictures and tapestries, and it was in the eighties and early nineties that he made his collection part of which forms the Iveagh Bequest for Kenwood.

The poor show made by Iveagh's furniture at Kenwood may now be explained. When he acquired Kenwood in 1925 Iveagh did not present it to the nation immediately. His stated intention was that it should become a museum after ten years or upon his death, whichever came sooner. In the event, only two years of his life remained. At the opening ceremony in 1928 his son revealed 'It had been the ambition of his father to arrange the pictures himself, but he died before he was able to do so' (*St Pancras Chronicle*, 20 July 1928). They were hung by Sir Charles Holmes. Had Iveagh enjoyed that lost decade at Kenwood, we may speculate that the finest pieces of furniture would have been transferred from Elveden, Dublin and Grosvenor Place. The collection of furniture would have stood the test of time far better, and look very different today.

## The changing collections

From the outset, the first furniture collection was recognised as inadequate company for the paintings. In an article announcing 'Lord Iveagh's Bequest' published in *Country Life* in November 1927 (eight months before Kenwood opened to the public) the author rejoiced 'Such a gift has not been made since the bequest of the Wallace Collection'. But the comparison stopped there, as he lamented 'It is unlikely, however, that the Iveagh collection will suffice to furnish all the rooms'.

Kenwood's first museum collection is recorded in early photographs and in the

*Furniture designed by Robert Adam for the Library, Hall and Parlour at Kenwood, as engraved for Robert and James Adam's* Works *(1774). Several of these pieces may be seen at Kenwood today (see page 29).*

inventory of 1930. These vividly evoke the Edwardian illusion of Georgian domestic life, with all its paraphernalia. In addition to a liberal distribution of mahogany side chairs and card tables, there were many items of no obvious relevance to the villa remodelled by Adam for the 1st Earl of Mansfield. Perhaps the most enigmatic references in the 1930 inventory are to '1 carved monkey wooden ornament' in the 'Boudoir', '1 Native drum' in the Orangery and '1 Treasure chest' in the East Hall.

Upstairs, the alcove bedroom was fully furnished as 'Her Ladyship's Bedroom', complete down to a seven-piece Minton toilet set, a towel horse and pin cushion, with twenty-three coloured engravings (mostly Malton's views of Dublin). Clearly, despite the intention of the Act to recreate the artistic home of an eighteenth-century gentleman, the practice of the Administrative Trustees was to present Kenwood as Lord and Lady Iveagh's home. Their approach is best illustrated by one of the first postcards produced, showing 'Lord Iveagh's Bedroom' (see page 41). The sixty-three items recorded in this room in the inventory even included '1 Electric kettle' which may have helped to convince visitors that Lord Iveagh slept here more often than the occasional weekend. The adjacent 'Bathroom' with its 'Coalport flowered toilet ware' had a bath, but tradition holds that it was never plumbed in.

This stage-like display of daily life survived, unruffled (but for the addition of further furniture from the Guinness family and the inevitable petty thefts) until Kenwood closed its doors shortly before the Second World War. Incredibly, the Edwardian museum remained within, as if in a time-capsule, still guarded by the house manager, Captain Roberts-Wray CB, OBE, VD, RNVR and the secretary and housekeeper, Miss Mary Tibbs. The paintings were removed to the National Portrait Gallery's own store, leaving empty frames hanging on the walls.

Eleven years later, in 1950, the house reopened under the London County Council, with its first curator, Loraine Conran, and Anthony Blunt as adviser. In order to launch Kenwood's tradition of summer exhibitions, Conran cleared away the bedrooms to create temporary display galleries, using the present lecture room as a vast furniture store, as is clear from his inventory of 1952. Most of the furnishings on the ground floor remained, somewhat rearranged and enhanced by new window curtains, but an acquisition policy evolved. This was developed from 1962 by the second curator, Alister Campbell, into the formation of a visual dictionary of Georgian furniture, with quality pieces arranged on low plinths. Under John Jacob, from 1967, the emphasis was placed squarely on fine paintings

*An armchair from the Moor Park suite, 1764.*

and Adam, particularly the furniture lost at the Kenwood sale in 1922.

The Adam period furniture collection to be enjoyed at Kenwood today comprises the original pieces that have 'come home' after detective work on both sides of the Atlantic, together with documented furniture from contemporary Adam houses, most notably Moor Park (to be seen in the Orangery) and Croome Court (to be seen in the Ante Chamber to the Library). There is no attempt to provide a survey of Adam's career as a designer of furniture, and the lighter, more elaborate pieces characteristic of his later style combining colours, marquetry and gilt ornament, will not be found at Kenwood. We cannot hope to refurnish the house fully as Adam intended: the earliest-known inventory dates from 1831, several pieces are preserved in the Mansfield family collection and the auction records from 1922 are inadequate. Moreover, Kenwood is now the home of a later collection of paintings, one of international importance, to which appropriate additions are occasionally made through gift and purchase.

## Jewellery, shoe buckles and miniatures

A sure indication of the public's love of Kenwood is the way the museum continues to attract gifts, not only of individual paintings and pieces of furniture, but of entire collections. These include eighteenth- and nineteenth-century jewellery presented by Mrs John Hull Grundy, nearly 1,300 Georgian shoe buckles from the collection formed by Lady Maufe, and British portrait miniatures from the collection of Marie Elizabeth Jane Irving Draper. These three collections are usually displayed in the upstairs rooms, and provide yet another reason to return to Kenwood.

*'Skeleton clock' by John Joseph Merlin, 1776. The earliest dated skeleton clock, it was designed as an eight-day movement with as few wheels as possible. Gainsborough's portrait of Merlin, 'the ingenious mechanick' may be seen at Kenwood.*

## *Chapter Five*
# THE PARK AND ESTATE

'The whole scene is amazingly gay, magnificent, beautiful and picturesque. The hill and dale are finely diversified; nor is it easy to imagine a situation more striking without, or more agreeably retired and peaceful within.' So wrote Robert Adam in 1774 of Kenwood and the 'extensive prospect' it commanded at that time 'of London, Greenwich Hospital, the River Thames, the ships passing up and down', framed on either side by 'the mountainous villages of Highgate and Hampstead'. The distant view is somewhat obscured today by the growth of trees, but the character of the 'whole scene' remains just as striking.

The history of the cultivated estate can be divided into three documented phases: the formal garden of the first half of the eighteenth century, as recorded in Rocque's map of 1745 (page 80); the more picturesque landscape from the 1st Earl of Mansfield's time, as painted (with some imagination) by John Wootton in 1755 (page 81); and the landscape remodelled by the 2nd Earl of Mansfield in 1793–6 and completed by the third Earl, largely to Humphry Repton's designs. But for the loss of some original footpaths, the removal of flower beds and the overgrowth of scrub, the gardens and parkland known to Repton and his patron essentially survive today, and provide a magnificent setting for the neoclassical villa.

Bordered on three sides by Hampstead Heath, the Kenwood estate has a different character from the Heath, having been maintained as a designed landscape until the 1950s. For nearly two hundred years it survived as a balanced collection of contrasts between grassland, woodland and wetland, interspersed with sudden surprises and features, particularly glimpses of the house and great vistas towards London. Taking the 'circuits', visitors may still enjoy this variety, passing through the picturesque, the beautiful and the sublime. In recent years, the contrasts became blurred, as over-competitive species took over and Kenwood began to resemble a 'wild' heath. Current restoration seeks a more balanced variety, so that wild flowers, trees, animals and wildfowl may all flourish, alongside the many Londoners who come to see the seasons change.

FACING PREVIOUS PAGE
*The house and estate from the
Wood Pond.*
PREVIOUS PAGE Caen Wood
*by John Greig, 1805 (detail)*

# THE
# FORMAL GARDEN

In the sixteenth century Kenwood was a woodland estate, commercially cultivated for its timber by a series of leaseholders; the original ponds (fed by headsprings of the Fleet River) were created as reservoirs for the residents of London. The first park was presumably laid out after the first house was built around 1616 by John Bill in his estate of some 460 acres (see chapter 3). All that remains from the seventeenth century is the terrace (probably created when the foundations for the house were dug, the excavated earth having been spread to level the hillside). The lime avenue (somewhat decimated by the hurricane of 16 October 1987) was first planted in 1729. Numerous foreign trees were planted by the Earl of Ilay's gardeners in the first half of the eighteenth century, and this love of 'exotics' was inherited by his nephew, the 3rd Earl of Bute.

John Stuart, 3rd Earl of Bute, lived at Kenwood from about 1747. He became King George III's prime minister, and was largely responsible for the creation of Kew Gardens. Rocque's map of 1745 records the estate he acquired from his father and uncle. Below the south front of 'Ken Wood House' formal gardens stretched down to four fish ponds; beyond lay 'KEN WOOD' itself, divided by three great avenues, ideal for horse riding. A substantial forecourt lay between the north front of the house and Hampstead Lane, with a kitchen garden to one side and scattered outbuildings to the other. The estate was framed by Hampstead Lane to the north, Millfield Lane to the east, a manorial ditch to the west and Ken Wood to the south.

In 1751 Bute described Kenwood to a colleague (probably the Dutch scholar Gronovius): 'to the south an old wood of 30 acres belonging to me; over which the whole city with 16 miles of the river appears from every window; a garden of 8 acres betwixt me and the wood I am filling with every exotick our climate will protect.' He also filled at least two volumes with observations on the plants on his English estate and made comparative studies between the rainfall at Kenwood and on his native Isle of Bute. Beyond planting, Bute seems to have made no substantial changes to the design of the estate.

In 1754 Bute sold Kenwood to his fellow Scot, William Murray, later 1st Earl of Mansfield. Under the first Earl the estate expanded from nearly 90 to 232 acres; ultimately it covered over 1,500 acres, stretching south past Highgate Ponds and Millfield Farm to Parliament Hill and Gospel Oak, and north beyond the present Hampstead and Highgate golf courses to today's A1 (Lyttleton Road). For all his noted patronage of Robert and James Adam, Lord Mansfield did not commission a landscape architect to remodel the grounds.

# THE PICTURESQUE
# GARDEN

The first Earl had been the protégé of Alexander Pope in his youth, and it is significant that for the first decade of his residence at Kenwood Lord Mansfield concentrated on the grounds rather than the house. We may assume that he followed Pope's advice to Lord Burlington to 'Consult the *Genius* of the *Place* in all', and respect the spirit of the landscape, rather than impose a foreign character upon it. Unfortunately no detailed plans have yet come to light.

The formal garden recorded in Rocque's map was soon swept away. The park was not simply returned to nature but 'improved', to provide a picturesque foreground for the fine prospect to be enjoyed from the house and terrace. There is little trace of this formal planting in Wootton's painting of 1755, and the four fish ponds are shown converted largely to their present appearance as two lakes. The 'Thousand Pound Pond' (first recorded as such

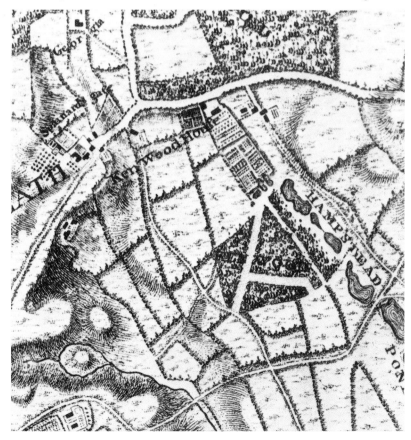

*A detail from John Rocque's* Plan of London, *1745, showing the Kenwood estate.*

'A View of the Ancient Bridge at
Kenwood' by Mrs Delany, 1757.
*The ancient bridge no longer
survives but the end of the stone
bridge may be seen on the left in
this drawing.*

in 1793) presumably takes its name from the great cost of its creation. Together with the Wood Pond it gives the illusion of a Thames-side setting, as if at Twickenham or Richmond. Wootton's view may be coloured by Mansfield's aspirations as much as by progress to date. No great lakes or grazing sheep are visible in Mrs Delany's finished drawings of 1756 and 1757 (although they do confirm the partial removal of flower beds in favour of lawn).

In making these changes Mansfield may have been carrying out Bute's own intentions, for the *Morning Herald & Daily Advertiser* noted in 1781 that 'the lawn and water, which form the scene from the house . . . have been worked according to the plan laid down and left by Lord Bute. The rest of the ground is altogether inartificial; grass and gravel walks through the wood. The extent of these walks is two miles.' There is no evidence of any landscape gardener working at Kenwood in these years. Lord Mansfield's faithful Land Steward, Edward Hunter, oversaw the improvements, and continued in post into the nineteenth century under the second and third Earls.

The 'sham bridge' completed the illusion of a flowing river, and would have helped to evoke memories of landscape paintings by Claude and Poussin. It is first recorded in 1786 and the following year, shortly before Lord Mansfield's retirement, a new boat was acquired for the lake. The bridge was rebuilt in 1791. Designs by Robert Adam for summer houses survive, and one may relate to 'Adam's Seat in Wood' recorded in the Kenwood Account Book. According to the diary of the Earl of Ailesbury,

when Mansfield was considering offering his resignation in 1780 he would walk a 'circuit' of some four or five miles around the estate each day from which he could admire great vistas towards the City, the Thames and Greenwich.

## HUMPHRY REPTON AT KENWOOD

The second Earl resided at Kenwood for just three years before his death in 1796, but in that time he enlarged the house, diverted Hampstead Lane to the other side of the North Wood, and built most of the farm, lodges, service wing and stables. In 1793 he commissioned the landscape architect Humphry Repton to prepare a 'Red Book' of proposals for Kenwood, with watercolour illustrations on flaps which could be raised to reveal Repton's schemes. Unfortunately this crucial document is still untraced.

Repton made at least three visits to Kenwood between 1793 and 1796; he had three surveys of the estate commissioned and he advised the second Earl's architect Nasmith, and his successor Saunders, on the building works. Repton also worked at the adjacent properties Fitzroy Farm and Evergreen Hill, so it seems likely that he conceived his designs for remodelling Kenwood in terms of a unified extensive landscape. Unlike 'Capability' Brown, he was no contractor, and his schemes would have been realised by Edward Hunter.

In 1796 Repton wrote to his deceased patron's executors after visiting Kenwood: 'I could hardly distinguish what was my plan from what had been altered.' Financial accounts reveal that the rival landscape gardener William Eames had been consulted briefly in 1795, but otherwise there is no evidence of another landscape gardener to whom the remodelling of Kenwood can be attributed. Features characteristic of Repton's work may still be recognised here today, particularly the ivy arbour with its breathtaking opening on to the terrace, lawns and lakes of Kenwood's natural amphitheatre. Equally unforgettable are Kenwood's winding rhododendron walks. The American rhododendrons, so often regarded as a 'Victorian' embellishment, were recorded flourishing here as early as 1806.

Other changes undertaken in the second Earl's time, and typical of Repton's work, include the twisting serpentine drive from the west lodge. This was conceived as the main approach route, and still passes by an old sandpit and under overhanging trees before emerging, suddenly, into the pool of light before the entrance portico. Less picturesque but equally characteristic of Repton is the more direct route from the east lodge, with its alternative branches leading to the service wing and stables.

The flower garden to the west of the house was created on the site of the old kitchen garden. When fully planted it would have completed the sequence of sudden contrasts between the west drive, the forecourt and the open parkland lying beyond the trellis arch. The view across the flower garden from the house was crowned by an ornamental dairy, built on a knoll to resemble a Swiss chalet. On the south front, the terrace was extended to link with the circuit around the estate. The parkland was planted with trees to break up the open expanse of lawn and to block the distant view of London. The general effect of these improvements was to create variety, contrast and surprise, in place of the expansive landscape with its grand prospect south towards London.

Among the estate's many admirers in these years was Samuel Taylor Coleridge. In 1817 he wrote to Henry Crabb Robinson, inviting him to dine in Highgate: 'The Day, the Dinner Hour, you may appoint yourself – but what I most wish would be . . . to walk or to be driven in Mr Gillman's Gig to Caen Wood & its delicious Groves and Alleys.'

# MR HUNTER, STEWARD

A vivid and often amusing picture of life on the estate is evoked by the correspondence between Mr Hunter and the third Earl in 1818, when the latter was in France. For example, on 18 May Hunter described to Lord Mansfield the following work undertaken at Kenwood: 'Garden . . . 6 men mowing till 9, after, 4 howing 3 digging 2 in flower garden. Man in wood. Fields: . . . 2 teams at plough, team carting dung. Man filling ditto. Man ditching. Man binding hay. Man with stooks.' Hunter was obliged to compile lengthy lists of the seeds and plants sent by the third Earl from France, many of which were unidentifiable, and dead on arrival. In addition to fine French furniture, bronzes, porcelain and wine, the third Earl sent lettuces from Versailles, German celery, vines, fruit and nut trees, wheat, dahlias, alpine strawberries and much more. Meanwhile Hunter writes, rather wearily, of staff shortages, the dangers of trying to feed pigs on boiled garden refuse, filling the ice house, brewing, and the problems of disposing of unexpected puppies, forever concluding his letters with the familiar phrase 'All Well at Kenwood'.

# J.C. LOUDON

The fullest published account of the Kenwood estate appeared in J. C. Loudon's *Suburban Gardener* (1838), just two years before the death of the third Earl. The author had previously worked at Mansfield's Scottish seat, Scone Palace. Admiring the work of recent generations, Loudon felt confident that 'This is, beyond all

*The trellis tunnel leading onto the terrace, as illustrated in J. C. Loudon's* The Suburban Gardener, *1838.*

question, the finest country residence in the suburbs of London, in point of natural beauty of the ground and wood, and in point also of the main features of art.' Many would agree today with his observation that 'as an example of peaceful sylvan beauty, nothing can surpass Kenwood'. He was convinced that 'it is, indeed, difficult to imagine a more retired or more romantic spot, and yet of such extent, so near a great metropolis'.

Loudon's accompanying plan indicated sheep pasture beyond a 'wire fence' below the terrace, and 'A broad terrace walk' of moss 'overhung by immense trees, on the outskirts of the park, and from some points in which magnificent views of London are obtained'. This walk included two paths through the south wood, one on the outer edge, affording fine prospects of London, the other on the inner side, giving views across the ponds to the house itself. The three views Loudon identified for highest praise, however, were those north from the portico, south from the terrace and west across the flower garden (from the veranda). Loudon had no love for this flower garden behind the lime avenue, which then contained 'too many small trees and shrubs among the flowers: in consequence of this, the turf is almost always damp . . . the flower-beds also, are too large . . .'. Most of the flower beds were finally removed in 1964, for ease of maintenance.

# PRESERVATION

The later Earls of Mansfield appear to have made only minor alterations to the landscape, and the estate known to Repton and Loudon essentially survives to this day. In 1889 the fourth Earl sold three of the Highgate Ponds plus Parliament Hill to the Metropolitan Board of Works and in 1914 the sixth Earl began to negotiate the sale of the remaining estate to a syndicate of builders. Fortunately the war postponed suburban development and the successful endeavours of the Kenwood Preservation Council and individuals raised funds to buy the ponds and the woods beyond. On 18 July 1925 King George V opened 121 acres of 'Ken Wood' to the public, and the same year Lord Iveagh purchased the house and surrounding 74 acres. The Iveagh Bequest opened to the public in 1928. The estate was administered first by the London County Council, then by the Greater London Council, and is now the responsibility of English Heritage, in collaboration with the Corporation of London.

Post-war additions to the park include the gate piers designed for Montagu House, 22

Portman Square, by Adam's great rival, James 'Athenian' Stuart, and Dr Johnson's Summer House (moved here from Streatham and opened in 1968). There are modern sculptures by Henry Moore, Barbara Hepworth, Reg Butler and others.

The historic character of the Kenwood estate has received special attention since 1986 when English Heritage became the Administrative Trustee of the Iveagh Bequest, Kenwood. English Heritage has a national responsibility for the protection of historic landscapes, and Kenwood is now listed Grade 2* in the Register of Parks and Gardens of Historic Interest compiled by English Heritage. Several areas of the estate are classified as being of Special Scientific Interest. Whilst continuing to maintain Kenwood as a public open space, English Heritage is committed to the partial restoration of the estate. The Iveagh Bequest (Kenwood) Act of Parliament of 1929 specifically endorses 'the first Lord Iveagh's wishes that the atmosphere of a gentleman's private park should be preserved'. Historic planting, paths and modern facilities are being improved with due respect for both the Act and the needs of today's public.

*Dr Johnson in his summer house at Streatham, 1773. The summer house was saved and re-erected at Kenwood in 1968.*

*The concert bowl.*

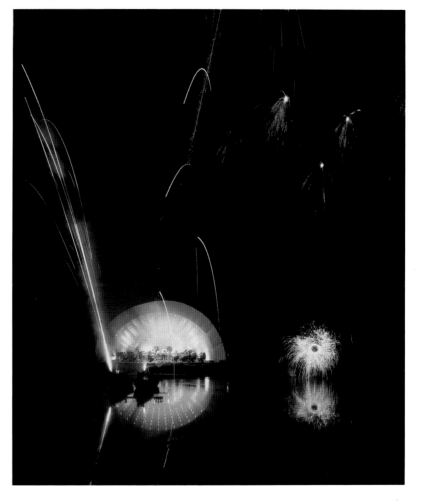

## Acknowledgements

This publication would not have been possible without the generous co-operation of Lord and Lady Mansfield and their staff at Scone Palace, particularly Dianne Cowan and Commander Robinson, and of Joan Auld, archivist at Dundee University. We gratefully acknowledge Lord Mansfield's permission to quote from documents in his family archive. Kenwood owes an immeasurable debt to Jacob Simon, who organized and greatly enriched the museum's archive when he was assistant curator. Among the many to whom thanks are due, we would particularly like to mention the following: David Beech, Carol Colson, Sebastian Edwards, Anne French, Gwynydd Gosling, Christine Higgs, Paul Highnam, Jeremy Hutchinson, John Jacob, George Levy, Christine Mathez, Georgina Mersh, Margaret Richardson, Sandra Salt, Raymond Smith and Andrew Wimble.

As editor and project manager Katy Carter saw the publication to fruition. Without the patience and understanding of Barbara and Maximilian Bryant, the text could not have been written. Finally we are indebted to Noel de Keyser and Vicky Naish of Savills plc, for negotiating the generous sponsorship of this publication.

## Further Reading

Robert and James Adam, *The Works in Architecture of Robert and James Adam*, I, no II (London, 1774).

Gene Adams, 'Dido Elizabeth Belle. A Black Girl at Kenwood', *Camden History Review*, 12 (1984), pp 10–14.

Anthony Blunt and Peter Murray, *The Iveagh Bequest, Kenwood, Catalogue of Paintings* (London, 1953).

Arthur T. Bolton, *The Architecture of Robert and James Adam* (London, 1922).

Julius Bryant, *Finest Prospects: Three Historic Houses*, exhibition catalogue (Kenwood, 1986).

Julius Bryant, 'Back as Adam intended: Adam furniture at Kenwood', *Country Life*, 3 November 1988, pp 192–5.

Alan Farmer, *Hampstead Heath* (New Barnet, 1984).

Edmund Heward, *Lord Mansfield* (London, 1979).

John Holliday, *The Life of William late Earl of Mansfield* (London, 1797).

Sir Charles Holmes, *Pictures from the Iveagh Bequest and Collections* (London, 1928).

London County Council, *Survey of London XVII: The Village of Highgate* (London, 1936).

J. C. Loudon, *The Suburban Gardener and Villa Companion* (London, 1838).

Frederick Mullally, *The Silver Salver. The story of the Guinness Family* (London, 1981).

John Richardson, *Highgate – Its History since the Fifteenth Century* (New Barnet, 1983).

Francis Russell, 'Portraits for Plutocrats: Georgian Portraiture and British Collectors 1870–1920', *Country Life*, 24 October 1985, pp 1264–6.

Jacob Simon, 'Humphry Repton at Kenwood: A Missing Red Book', *Camden History Review*, 11 (1984), pp 4–9.

John Summerson, *The Iveagh Bequest, Kenwood: A Short Account of its History and Architecture* (London, 1953).

## Join English Heritage

The Iveagh Bequest, Kenwood, is one of four eighteenth-century historic houses in London which are cared for by English Heritage. The others are Chiswick House, Marble Hill House, Twickenham, and Ranger's House, Blackheath.

You can support the work of English Heritage, and enjoy special privileges and benefits, by becoming a member. Your membership card grants free admission to all English Heritage properties where an entrance fee is charged. Ask for details at any of our staffed properties, or, by post only, from English Heritage Membership Department, PO Box 1BB, London W1A 1BB.

## London Historic House Museums Trust

The Trust was established in 1987 to raise funds for projects and acquisitions at the four historic house museums in London in the care of English Heritage. Donations of any size are most welcome. The Trust is registered as a charity (no 295386) and can therefore recover income tax deducted from donations made by way of covenant. For further details of the Trust together with forms of covenant, banker's orders, etc, please write to the London Historic House Museums Trust, c/o The Iveagh Bequest, Kenwood.

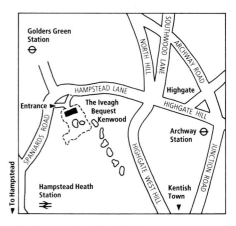

## Information for Visitors

The Iveagh Bequest, Kenwood
Hampstead Lane
London NW3 7JR

Open: Good Friday or 1 April (whichever is earlier) to 30 Sept, daily 10am – 6pm; 1 Oct to Maunday Thursday or 31 March (whichever is earlier), daily 10am – 4pm; closed 24 – 25 Dec.
House: 01-348 1286
Restaurant: 01-341 5384
Concerts: 01-973 3472.